BANK NOTES

BANK NOTES

An Inside Look at the
Launching of North Carolina's
Banking Ascendancy

— AND —

a Commentary on the Current
New World of Banking

LUTHER H. HODGES, JR.

PHOENIX PRESS   BLOWING ROCK, NORTH CAROLINA

Design and production by BW&A Books, Inc.

ISBN: 978-0-9976558-0-3 (paperback)

ISBN: 978-0-9976558-1-0 (cloth)

Bank Notes is dedicated to my children, Anne Houston Hodges Predieri and Luther Hartwell Hodges, III. I was far too busy moving up the banking ladder in their early years, so full credit for their development rests with their mother, Dorothy Duncan Hodges. I do rejoice in their professional success in the economic and banking professions. Their accomplishments in today's financial services industry give me great pride; indeed, their contributions to the final chapter of *Bank Notes* are a welcome addition to my comments on the "new world of banking."

CONTENTS

Introduction   ix

A Brief Look at North Carolina
Banking History   1

My Banking Career   17

Reflections on Bank Regulation
and the Future of Banking   47

Appendix   67

Introduction

By the end of the twentieth century, North Carolina was home to two of the world's major banks, and its largest city, Charlotte, was one of the world's most important financial centers. That status represented a truly astonishing transformation. Less than fifty years earlier, commercial banking in North Carolina consisted mostly of small local institutions, and only a few banks in the state had branches other than their headquarters office.

The spectacular ascent of the state's leading banks was a major factor in transforming North Carolina from an economy based at mid-century on tobacco farms and textile mills—both facing unpromising futures—to one built on financial services, research, technology, and medicine.

The rapid growth of those small Southern banks was fundamentally based on the demographics of the region and the audacious vision of several young bank executives. For a few years in the 1960s and 1970s, I was one of those young bankers.

What follows is based on my experiences in those years in North Carolina, along with an intimate view of bank regulation as experienced by The National Bank of Washington. These recollections and reflections provide some interesting insights into the circumstances, personalities, and strategies that launched North Carolina's major banks into the stratosphere and pushed the state's economy into the twenty-first century. Finally, I try to outline a future for the banking industry over the decades to come. Moreover, the sad story of the failure in 1990 of The National Bank of Washington provides insight into regulatory misdeeds which today face many banks. The new world of banking threatens all banks' ability to succeed and grow in the face of overwhelming new banking regulations.

A Brief Look at
North Carolina Banking History

North Carolina in the middle years of the twentieth century was a relatively poor, largely rural state without a city of any real regional, much less national, significance. In those days, no one would have predicted that by the end of the century two of its homegrown banks would be among the nation's largest, and Charlotte would rank as at least the second-most important banking center in America and one of the most important in the world.

The paradox is simply that the rural character of the state, and the lack of a true urban center at mid-century, were the primary reasons the state became home to two of the giants of commercial banking. Basically North Carolina, unlike other states, did not prohibit or restrict branch banking. Elsewhere, state laws against bank expansion across municipal or county boundaries were enacted to protect small-town banks against competition from larger banks in major cities. In a state with little wealth and no large urban center, North Carolina's legislators had never seen any need for such restrictions on branch banking. A few comparative figures from the 1950 census may clarify this issue.

In 1950, New York City was home to more than half its state's population. Chicago represented more than a third of the population of Illinois. In Maryland, almost 40 percent of the population lived in Baltimore. Even in many less urban states, major cities accounted for a significant percentage of the population: 9 percent of Floridians in Miami, for example, and 6 percent of Texans in Dallas.

Closer to home, 7 percent of Virginians lived in Richmond, and 6 percent in Norfolk. Memphis accounted for 12 percent of the population of Tennessee. Atlanta held almost 10 percent of the Georgia population.

In contrast, North Carolina's largest city, Charlotte, had a population of about 135,000, only about 3 percent of the state.

The percentage of population characterized as urban in neighboring states was 45 percent in Georgia, 47 percent in Virginia, 55 percent in Tennessee, and 35 percent in South Carolina. Only 33.7 percent of North Carolina's population was considered urban, and much of that population was in small to medium-size towns.

Marginal rural poverty defined eastern and western North Carolina, with low-wage industry the primary economic sector in the Piedmont. With a population that was the most homogeneous of any state in the union in the 1950s and dispersed mostly across rural areas and small towns, North Carolina experienced very little of the friction found in many other states between urban and rural, richer and poorer, or large cities and small towns. Few, if any, lawmakers or other influential citizens in North Carolina in the 1940s or 1950s considered "big city" banks a threat to hometown institutions, so there was no effective constituency for prohibitions on branch banking.

The freedom to expand geographically represented a critical opportunity for a few relatively small banks with large ambitions. Branch banking across city limits and county lines was the first small step toward eventual interstate banking and national stature for aggressive North Carolina banks.

Wachovia Bank and Trust Company

The first institution to take significant advantage of North Carolina's freedom was Wachovia Bank and Trust Company in Winston-Salem. Wachovia National Bank opened in 1879 in Winston, North Carolina. North Carolina's first trust company, Wachovia Loan and Trust Company, was founded in Winston in 1893. Those two institutions merged to create Wachovia Bank and Trust Company in 1911. Two years later, Winston and the adjacent Moravian village of Salem merged to form the city of Winston-Salem. That same year, the new city's largest employer, R. J. Reynolds Tobacco Company, launched Camel cigarettes, which became the best-selling brand in America.

As the hometown bank of R. J. Reynolds Tobacco, Wachovia Bank and Trust opened with deposits of $4 million, capital stock of $1.25 million, and total resources of $7 million and was ranked as the largest bank in the South. It remained the largest bank in North Carolina for the next sixty years.

From its Winston-Salem base, Wachovia reached east to High Point, where the Southern Furniture Manufacturers Association had been founded in 1911; to Greensboro, where the Cone brothers' White Oak Cotton Mills had recently become the world's largest manufacturer of a sturdy work-clothes fabric called denim; to Durham, home of James B. Duke's American Tobacco Company; and on to Raleigh, the state capital. Wachovia's Raleigh offices gave the bank a foothold to compete for deposits from state government and the tobacco fields to the east. Wachovia also was expanding to the south, through the textile towns of the southern Piedmont and all the way to Charlotte, which had passed Wilmington as the state's largest city with a 1910 census count of more than 34,000.

As the state's most powerful financial institution, with offices in the capital, Wachovia also began to develop and increase its political influence. Robert M. Hanes, who became president in 1931 and headed the bank for twenty-five years, enjoyed unparalleled influence in state politics, as did his successors, Archie Davis, who became chairman in 1956, and John Watlington, who was named president and chief executive officer the same year.

A digression: Over the years many people have been curious about the name Wachovia. Many North Carolinians probably assume the name is derived from a Native American word, but Wachovia is of German origin. "Wach" was a stream and "au" means meadowland. In 1753, when Moravian settlers bought about 100,000 acres in the North Carolina Piedmont just east of the Yadkin River, they called the land "Wachau" in honor of Count Nicholas Ludwig von Zinzendorf. The count, in 1722, invited a Protestant Christian group fleeing persecution in Moravia to settle on his estate. The Moravians thought their new land in North Carolina resembled the count's ancestral home in the Wachau Valley of Austria, and over time, the name of the Moravian settlement in North Carolina evolved into its English form, Wachovia.

The bank with the intriguing German-Moravian name was clearly the dominant institution in commercial banking in North Carolina through the first half of the twentieth century, although several other banks emerged to be significant in their regions of the state. One was Branch Banking and Trust (now BB&T), founded in Wilson in the late nineteenth century. Another was First Citizens Bank and Trust Company, which began as the Bank of Smithfield in 1898 and has been owned and successfully managed over the years by the Holding family.

NCNB and First Union Bank

A bit later, and perhaps more important, were the modest beginnings of two banks in Charlotte. One was Southern States Trust Company, established in a Tryon Street storefront in 1900 by Word H. Wood and George H. Stephens. In 1906 they changed the name of the bank to American Trust Company. In 1908, H. M. Victor set up a desk in the lobby of the Buford Hotel, also on Tryon Street, and called the business Union National Bank.

From those small Tryon Street beginnings grew the institutions—North Carolina National Bank and First Union National Bank—that fifty years later began to seriously challenge Wachovia for the position of the state's largest bank. Serious competition would also bring new, ambitious talent into the management of the state's leading banks. Their leadership and vision, along with legislative and regulatory changes and the impact of historic social upheavals, would transform the character, personality, and national and international significance of banking in North Carolina.

In 1905, a year before Southern States Trust Company changed its name to American Trust Company, seventeen-year-old Torrence Eli Hemby was hired as a "runner" for the bank. One of Hemby's tasks was to visit small-town banks across the Piedmont and establish correspondent bank relationships with American Trust. In 1943 he was named president of American Trust Company, and eight years later, approaching retirement age and scouting for a successor, he recruited a Baltimore banker and former FDIC bank examiner named Addison Hardcastle Reese.

With Hemby as chairman of the board and Addison Reese as president, the American Trust Company negotiated a series of mergers that created North Carolina National Bank and generated the momentum that eventually would transform the Charlotte bank into one of the nation's major financial institutions. Fifty years later, few people recognize that the father of today's Charlotte-based Bank of America was actually Addison H. Reese.

In 1957, American Trust Company merged with an older and more retail Charlotte institution, Commercial National Bank, which had been established by Major Clement Dowd in 1874, predating even Wachovia. The merger created the American Commercial Bank, which quickly acquired First National Bank of Raleigh.

A block away, under the leadership of Carl McCraw, Sr., Charlotte's Union National Bank merged in 1958 with Asheville's First National Bank & Trust Company, combining two very successful local franchises and creating First Union National Bank. In its effort to compete with long-dominant Wachovia, First Union completed a number of smaller mergers in the state in the early 1960s and, in 1964, acquired the Cameron-Brown Company, a Raleigh mortgage banking firm. The acquisition gave First Union not only a very successful mortgage banking operation but also a major addition of executive talent in Charles Clifford Cameron, a founder and president of Cameron-Brown. Cliff Cameron was quickly named executive vice president of First Union.

But the real challenge to Wachovia's dominance was the marriage of the American Commercial Bank and Greensboro's Security National Bank in the summer of 1960. Since the Depression, Greensboro's largest financial institution, the Jefferson Standard Life Insurance Company, had owned the Security National Bank, which had offices in other towns in Piedmont North Carolina in addition to Tarboro and Wilmington in eastern North Carolina. Jefferson Standard's sister corporation, Pilot Life Insurance Company in Greensboro, owned the Guilford National Bank. The management of the insurance companies merged their two banks under the name of Security National, which quickly acquired Depositors National Bank of Durham and then sought a major partner to create a serious competitor to Wachovia. Indeed, the searching for a partner was really an effort by the directors of Jefferson Standard to find adequate management for the life insurance company's banking assets. The directors identified this management in Charlotte's American Commercial Bank, and as a result Greensboro lost its banking headquarters. Many residents of Greensboro had some resentment toward Charlotte and NCNB, which, fortunately, passed some fifty years later.

Actually, there were a number of areas of rivalry between Charlotte and Greensboro, then the state's two largest cities, and the merger of 1960 was negotiated at the Holiday Inn in Salisbury, an important manufacturing town equidistant between the two cities. American Commercial Bank and Security National Bank chose to merge under the name North Carolina National Bank, which shortly became known as NCNB, and to locate its headquarters in Charlotte with Addison Reese as the chairman of the board and chief executive officer.

The new bank opened with forty branches across North Carolina, and subsequent mergers and acquisitions created a true statewide bank, the second-largest in the state. NCNB remained number two in size until 1972, when it surpassed Wachovia in total assets. First Union in Charlotte, then under the strong leadership of Cliff Cameron, remained number three. First Citizens Bank and Trust Company, headquartered in Raleigh, was number four. By 1972, banking assets in North Carolina had become quite significant, but the national success of the state's commercial banking giants was just beginning.

One-Bank Holding Companies

Commercial banking assumed a larger role in the economy and found new opportunities for creative growth in the late 1960s with the establishment of one-bank holding companies. In addition to its bank, a one-bank holding company could own and control, under existing regulation from the Federal Reserve System, companies offering a wider range of financial services, such as mortgage banking, factoring, and investment management. Since a one-bank holding company was not limited to a bank's customer deposits as a source of money to lend, the bank could leverage its operations with the assets and credit of affiliated companies and could borrow money by issuing corporate debt in the capital markets. The list of permissible activities initially included insurance agencies, but serious lobbying by the insurance industry deleted that opportunity in the early 1970s. At that time the holding company, NCNB Corporation, was forced to sell its American Commercial Insurance Agency.

Several North Carolina banks were quick to take advantage of the opportunity to form one-bank holding companies. First Union Corporation became the second one-bank holding company in the United States when it was established in 1967. NCNB Corporation and Wachovia Corporation were formed in 1968, and NCNB Corporation was the first to sell its debt, as "commercial paper," which helped finance its rapid expansion.

Interstate banking, however, was still prohibited by state and federal laws despite many efforts over the years to eliminate that prohibition. Fear of the concentration of power seems to be inherent in the American character. In any event the banking industry itself had never been united in support of interstate banking. The nation's largest banks, particularly in New York City, opposed interstate banking because it might permit—as it eventually did—strong regional banks to expand and compete with them in size and significance. Small-town or "country" banks also were opposed, because they did not want the giant banks to establish operations in their communities and compete for business. Only the regional banks, such as Wachovia, NCNB and First Union, believed they had something to gain with interstate banking.

The Growth Environment in North Carolina

The freedom of North Carolina banks to branch out across the state was a fundamental key to their early and continuing progress. But there were several other factors that contributed significantly to the kind of environment necessary for the extraordinary growth they experienced in the last quarter of the century.

One major development was Governor Luther Hodges' emphasis, in the mid-1950s, on economic development and attracting new and diverse industries to the state, setting a pattern that every North Carolina governor since has followed, as well as many later governors across the South. Such efforts were not as obviously benign, or as universally accepted, as might be thought today. In fact, some of the existing industries, such as textile and furniture manufacturers, did not like the idea of companies in other industries moving into the state and competing in the North Carolina labor market, particularly if they offered higher wages. The governor, a former textile executive, appreciated and supported the state's basic industries. But he knew that North Carolina's future prosperity would require a larger and more diversified industrial base, and he reached out across the nation and around the world to bring more jobs, and a greater diversity of jobs, to the state. That effort, and similar efforts by his successors, created new and growing markets for commercial banking services and an economic climate in which the state's banks could grow and thrive.

A closely related factor was Governor Hodges' vision of a research park to attract leading-edge research institutions and research-based corporations to the area defined by the state capital and three of its great universities—the University of North Carolina at Chapel Hill, North Carolina State University, and Duke University.

Then there was the explosive issue of racial segregation and civil rights which had been simmering for a number of years, and which Southern states and most Southern white people had tried to ignore. The U.S. Supreme Court declared racial segregation in public schools unconstitutional in May 1954, and less than six months later, in November, Gov. William B. Umstead died and Lieutenant Governor Hodges became governor. North Carolina's public schools were segregated by race, of course, so the court decision and the unavoidable question of whether and how to obey the law were on the governor's desk when Hodges moved into the office.

Many governors and other political leaders across the South pledged to defy the court's order and to maintain segregated schools. By the time Hodges was elected to a full term in 1956, many Southern elected officials and candidates for office were united under the cause of "massive resistance" to the court order, a term attributed at that time to U.S. Senator Harry Byrd of Virginia.

While other Southern governors vowed to preserve segregation and stand in schoolhouse doors to keep black students out, Governor Hodges calmly appointed a group of citizens, which became known as the Pearsall Committee, to devise a plan to deal with the desegregation order. The result was a proposed amendment to the Constitution of North Carolina that would allow the legislature to revise compulsory school attendance laws. After the amendment was overwhelmingly approved by North Carolina voters, the legislature enacted changes to allow white families to avoid sending their children to school with black students.

The Pearsall Committee was all white, and the Pearsall Plan was found unconstitutional when it was tested in the courts a few years later. But in contrast to the responses elsewhere in the South, the plan appeared moderate, attempting to quietly cir-

13

cumvent the court order without screaming defiance. The plan gave the state's white majority, virtually all of whom favored continued segregation, a reassuring sense that they had some control over what was going to happen to their children and the schools.

Most importantly, the plan bought the state and its people some time, which turned out to be critical. The high court had not ordered schools desegregated immediately, but with "all deliberate speed," which across the South turned out to be many years. By the time local school districts were faced with specific court orders to implement specific desegregation plans, most North Carolinians had accepted token desegregation based on neighborhood housing patterns, and some citizens were ready to accept more.

Governor Hodges' refusal to demagogue the issue established a climate in which his successor, Terry Sanford, could appoint local biracial committees to work for better race relations across the state even as school systems wrestled with the order to desegregate.

Meanwhile, to the rest of the nation, including corporate executives looking for new plant sites or headquarters reloca-tions, North Carolina appeared more moderate, more civilized, and more progressive than many other Southern states, an image which minimized potential damage to its economic development.

Even more forthright and assertive in seeking to avoid eco-nomically damaging fallout from racial friction was Mayor Stan-ford R. Brookshire of Charlotte. When he took office in 1961, racial confrontations in some other Southern cities were turn-ing violent, and the resulting images were playing on television screens across the nation. As a staunch Methodist, Brookshire was beginning to believe that racial segregation was wrong, at least as a matter of law and at least in places otherwise open to the public. As a businessman and former Chamber of Commerce president, the mayor realized that trying to maintain a segregated community was going to be very bad for business and a serious handicap to his city's economic ambitions.

In the spring of 1963, under Brookshire's urging, the Chamber of Commerce executive committee, and later its full board of directors, approved a resolution recommending "that all businesses in this community catering to the general public be opened immediately to all customers without regard to race, creed or color." Within the next few weeks, at the suggestion of a young cafeteria operator named James "Slug" Claiborne, who would later become one of the state's most successful restaurateurs, white business and civic leaders began inviting black business and professional men to lunch at Charlotte restaurants. Thus most of Charlotte's public accommodations voluntarily desegregated many months before Congress ordered them to do so.

In 1965, with support from Brookshire and the white business community, Fred Alexander, a soft-spoken black funeral director, was elected to the Charlotte City Council at a time when all council members were still elected at-large.

A few years later, after the Charlotte-Mecklenburg schools had permitted some desegregation of neighborhood schools, the federal court ordered the system to fully integrate every school by any means necessary, including crosstown busing. While the school board and the court wrestled over how this was to be accomplished, a group of citizens came up with a pupil assignment plan that the board and the court accepted. With a few minor exceptions, the changes were implemented peacefully, and for more than a quarter-century the people and leadership of Charlotte and Mecklenburg County could boast of having the finest fully integrated public school system in the United States.

Once again North Carolina, and particularly its largest city, were polishing the image of a place willing to give up old prejudices and discredited traditions in pursuit of progress, prosperity, and economic opportunity.

The impact of those factors is not as measurable as the number of branch offices established by a bank or the number of jobs created by a new factory, but it was profoundly positive for economic development and commercial banking in North Carolina. It is hard to imagine Charlotte becoming an international banking center by the end of the century if the city and state had taken a different direction at the fork which history had put in their path.

My Banking Career

Getting Started

My banking career began with a brief stay at one of North Carolina's two largest banks and continued at the other one for fifteen years.

In 1960, after completing my service in the United States Navy and my first year at Harvard Business School, I had a summer job with Wachovia Bank and Trust Company. I was acquainted with several senior officers at Wachovia through contacts in college and friends of my father, then governor of North Carolina and later secretary of commerce in the Kennedy administration. Wachovia's headquarters were in Winston-Salem, but my summer job was in Charlotte, which was convenient because my wife, Dot, and I were living at her parents' home in Monroe and expecting our first child, Anne Houston Hodges.

The job was primarily a learning experience and entailed working with a number of executives in the Charlotte office. I spent much of my time with Vice President Hugh Gentry, who was handling correspondent banking in South Carolina. We did a lot of traveling in that state, and I learned a great deal, enough even to write a second-year required paper at Harvard on "Establishing an International Department in a Regional Bank."

I also wrote a lengthy letter, expressing my appreciation and describing my experiences at the bank. My letter was addressed to the two senior officers at Wachovia who had arranged for my summer employment. The gratitude was genuine, but the letter was also an effort by a very young man to impress the bank executives with his insight, confidence, and candor. The term "corporate culture" did not exist at the time, but my impression that summer was that Wachovia was not a very "open" society. Indeed, there was not much incentive or reward for entrepreneurial thinking. Almost everyone was of the same mold and tethered to headquarters in Winston-Salem. I tried to convey that impression as politely as I could, thinking I might be helpful:

> As I prepare to close, let me just refer to what, I am sure, is a major question in every Wachovia executive's mind—namely, the degree of centralization, or decentralization, that will best permit each office to prosper within the general framework of a growing Wachovia Bank and Trust Company. There are, of course, numerous advantages in permitting the local officers to administer their own houses and, similarly, elements of control and conformity which demand central authority. I do not pretend to have an answer that satisfies both sides, but my view of the Credit Department in Charlotte, where numerous loans exceeding $100,000 come under heavy control, did indicate that the image of Winston-Salem frequently loomed too large in the administration of local affairs. Possibly I should avoid the subject of Winston-Salem versus Charlotte, for more thought than I could ever offer has determined the existing, comparatively decentralized system, and, further, I will be the first to acknowledge that criteria must be established and met for proper credit and administrative procedures. But I have viewed a problem, and I am now merely reflecting on this point so that I can more fully appreciate the situation. I certainly do not question the standards—only the idea that people must be afraid of them.

I later learned that this letter, intended to be constructive, was not appreciated. It would have been interesting to find out what kind of reception I would have had if I had later applied for a permanent job at Wachovia Bank.

The summer job at Wachovia in Charlotte gave me an oppor-tunity to take a look at North Carolina National Bank, an institution created by the merger in the summer of 1960 of Charlotte's American Commercial Bank and Greensboro's Security National Bank. Whiteford Blakeney, a Charlotte attorney and one of my many cousins, said that I should meet some people at "his" bank. He took me to the site of the former American Commercial Bank at Tryon and Fourth streets, where banking business was being conducted while the new North Carolina National Bank (NCNB) building was under construction. That building, which opened the following year, was the first glass skyscraper in North Carolina and the tallest building erected in Charlotte in the 1960s. Its shape and surface, strikingly contemporary for its time and place, made it an appropriate symbol for an aggressive, future-oriented bank. At eighteen stories, it stood a notch above the fifteen-story Wachovia Building, completed three years ear-lier a diagonal block away. The twelve-story, 1953-vintage First Union Building was across Tryon and one block to the south.

My cousin introduced me to Julian J. Clark, one of the state's best-known and most widely respected bankers, who was an executive vice president of the North Carolina National Bank, soon to be called NCNB. The meeting was most cordial, and I also met Addison Reese, the chairman and CEO. I learned later that Reese asked his new executive vice president, Thomas I. Storrs, then based in Greensboro, to stay in touch with me.

In 1961, after graduation from Harvard Business School, I could not decide whether to come home to North Carolina and look for a job in the banking business or go to New York City to work for a management consulting firm where I had enjoyed several employment interviews. I had earlier concluded that unless your family owned a textile or furniture company, no seri-ous business opportunity existed in North Carolina other than commercial banking. Before reaching a decision, I spent a year teaching at the business school of my alma mater, the University of North Carolina, and renting my father's recently purchased but still vacant retirement home in Chapel Hill.

One day that fall, the house's previous owner, George Watts Hill, was visiting with my father, and he asked what I wanted to do in life. I mentioned my interest in banking and asked his opinion of Wachovia versus North Carolina National Bank as an employer. He immediately responded and, to my surprise, did not mention his own Central Carolina Bank in Durham. He said: "Robert Hanes of Wachovia was North Carolina's banker of the 1950s, and Addison Reese of North Carolina National Bank would be that banker for the 1960s." In essence, he readily stated that NCNB represented the better opportunity for me. I took his advice.

Tom Storrs, then in charge of retail banking, was staying in touch with me, as Addison Reese had asked him to do. During my teaching year he would drop by Chapel Hill from time to time as he visited branch offices around the state. Near the end of my faculty term, Tom Storrs offered me a job with NCNB at an annual salary of $7,200, a nice increase over the $4,800 that I earned in the academic world.

Storrs was then in his middle forties. I later learned he had gone to work at the Federal Reserve Bank of Richmond as a teenager, after his father suffered financial and health problems during the Great Depression. He continued in the Federal Reserve System over a span of some twenty-six years, periodically interrupted long enough to earn a bachelor's degree at the University of Virginia and a master's and doctorate in economics at Harvard. He served as an officer in the Navy during World War II and was recalled to active duty during the Korean War.

The first NCNB building was completed in 1962.

In 1959 Tom Storrs was in charge of the Federal Reserve Bank in Charlotte; Addison Reese hired him as an executive vice president of North Carolina National Bank the following year. Storrs was clearly an intelligent, hard-working executive, and he knew that he was one of the candidates to succeed Addison Reese when he retired some twelve years in the future. In that year Storrs was responsible for NCNB's many branches, so he was quite busy introducing himself to all employees. He was personable enough, but one did not readily relate to him in any warm, supporting fashion.

As I had seriously considered a job in management consulting with the New York firm of Cresap, McCormick, and Paget, I was most pleased, upon my joining the bank on June 17, 1962, to learn that Addison Reese had just hired the same New York consulting firm to conduct a major compensation survey. My first assignment was to travel with the consultant to all of NCNB's branch offices and meet with most bank officers as we drew organizational charts and established consistent salary grades for all major positions. Mine was a great opportunity to get to know people throughout the organization and to get a better overall picture of what was, for its time, already a sprawling company with offices throughout the Piedmont area of North Carolina, plus Tarboro and Wilmington in the East.

Working with the consultants, I began to understand why George Watts Hill had said that Addison Reese would be the banker of the 1960s. Reese was a member of the last generation of business executives who could reach that level of achievement and authority in the corporate world without the benefit of a college degree. As head of NCNB, Reese would be in charge of at least two Harvard MBAs—John A. (Jack) Tate, Jr., and myself—plus one person with a Harvard doctorate in economics—Tom Storrs—plus countless others with advanced degrees in business, finance, and economics from other universities. Reese himself had dropped out of Johns Hopkins University after three years and performed manual labor before he was hired as a statistician by a private banking firm in Baltimore.

Addison Reese was later a bank examiner for the newly formed Federal Deposit Insurance Corporation. During World War II he served as an officer in the Army Air Corps, and then became president of a bank in his home state of Maryland. From there he moved to Charlotte as vice president and director of the American Trust Company, one of the forerunners of NCNB.

Reese was impressive in person—tall, handsome, good-humored, and gracious. He was a shrewd but friendly and courteous negotiator. As a boss, he was unfailingly considerate and commanded respect without being overbearing. Most important, perhaps, was his vision: the ambition and ability to imagine NCNB as a major national and international financial institution. Addison Reese was a most knowledgeable banker and clearly well respected in the entire banking community. In the 1960s he was elected president of the Association of Reserve City Bankers, a prestigious group of major bankers whose institutions were located in each of the twenty-four cities of the U.S. Federal Reserve System. On occasion, I was asked to write speeches for Addison Reese. Frankly, I was devoted to him and blessed my good fortune to have had an early assignment that placed me in the presence of the CEO. As years passed, I regularly noted that Addison H. Reese had been my mentor.

When I arrived at NCNB, Reese already had a strong management group in place: Julian Clark, the chief credit officer, whom I had first met while working with our principal competitor; Patrick N. Calhoun, the former president of the Guilford National Bank in Greensboro and an alumnus of the then Chase Manhattan Bank; Jack Tate, the head of marketing; Herbert Wayne,

The NCNB Corporation's 1973 Annual Report featured this portrait of retiring CEO Addison Reese.

the chief operating officer; and Ben Bostick, the head of all trust activity. But Reese was already planning so that the next generation of management would be ready when he and other leaders of that time began to retire and the bank continued to expand.

Early in my tenure at NCNB, Reese's other major project employing consultants was a leadership development program using the Greensboro firm now known as Farr & Associates. Twelve to fifteen young bank officers were assigned to meet with the consultant every week for more than a year. Out of that project two of us would climb rather rapidly to the top level of management at North Carolina National Bank. The other was the now legendary Hugh L. McColl, Jr.

Youth, Ambition, and Competition

I had known Hugh McColl at UNC-Chapel Hill, where we were enrolled in the Naval Reserve Officers Training Program and in the same graduating class. After we became commissioned officers in June 1957, Hugh spent two years with the Marines. He joined the American Commercial Bank in 1959 through the introduction of his father, a banker in Bennettsville, South Carolina, who was a good customer of the Charlotte bank. I served abroad on a ship in the Navy and returned to the United States to enter Harvard Business School in 1959. After I joined NCNB in 1962, Hugh and I became close friends and, indeed, we were very close business partners (and tennis partners) at the bank for over a decade.

Hugh was an exceptionally smart banker. I always attributed his ability to quickly analyze any quantitative issue to his experience of playing poker at his fraternity house during college. In any event, we were a good team because of his quantitative skills and leadership abilities and my interpersonal skills and ability to foresee many changes and opportunities.

It is hard to conceive that two young men in their thirties would have such visions of the future, but we both were thrust into an industry that had not recruited officers since prior to the Great Depression and World War II, and as the earlier generation retired, a great age gap existed between it and the succeeding generation. Moreover, we both were traveling bankers at the time, and we were the youngest members of the prestigious Association of Reserve City Bankers. For our age we were blessed with opportunity and firsthand knowledge of our rapidly changing industry.

Of course we were not the only visionary and ambitious young bankers in a city where bank towers increasingly dominated the skyline. Another particularly impressive young bank executive was Edward E. Crutchfield, just down the street at First Union National Bank. Ed had played tackle on Albemarle High School's 1958 state championship football team, gone to college at nearby Davidson, and joined First Union after earning his master's degree at the Wharton School of Finance in 1965.

Hugh and I tried to convince Crutchfield to join us at NCNB. We asked him, in effect, whether he "wouldn't rather play for the Yankees" than be the one star on a lesser team. Apparently he realized that the executive ladder at NCNB could get pretty crowded if he got on it, and he decided it would be easier to get to the top somewhere else. It turned out to be a good decision for him. In 1974 he became president of First Union, under Chairman Cliff Cameron. Just thirty-two years old, he was the youngest president of a major bank in the United States.

In 1971 Tom Storrs became president of NCNB and its holding company, NCNB Corporation, making him the designated successor to Addison Reese, who was anticipating his own retirement in 1974. But Storrs' impatience with less quick-witted colleagues and employees, plus a sometimes icy formality, were still possible obstacles to that succession. As president, Tom Storrs chose to have a management team of four—himself, Hugh, and me as vice chairmen of the bank, and William H. Dougherty as vice chairman of the holding company. Each of us, however, had responsibilities in both the bank and the holding company. For example, Hugh was in charge of the wholesale bank and a couple of other subsidiaries, and I was in charge of retail banking, certain staff units, and a couple of subsidiaries. Dougherty, a University of Pittsburgh graduate who had been a CPA with Price Waterhouse & Company, continued to serve as chief financial officer and was responsible for major operating and financial staff units.

BUSINESSMEN IN THE NEWS

DOUGHERTY, HODGES AND McCOLL OF NCNB

In late 1973, NCNB Corporation Chairman Addison H. Reese retired and was succeeded by North Carolina National Bank President Thomas I. Storrs. Speculation ran strong in the business community as to Mr. Storrs' successor as the parent company's and the bank's second-in-command. The answer was three men, all of whom are profiled in this month's Businessman in the News feature.

Luther H. Hodges, Jr.

By any yardstick, Luther H. Hodges, Jr., ranks high among the nation's youthful achievers. *Time* magazine's yardstick certainly assigned him a lofty measurement: last year the publication ranked him among its list of 200 emerging leaders in the United States.

With nearly six months remaining before he reaches age 40, Mr. Hodges is in his third year as chairman of the board of North Carolina National Bank. He oversees NCNB Financial Services, Inc., and sits as a member of the parent NCNB Corporation's board of directors. And he is chairman of the subsidiary Tri-South Corporation. As one of the financial institution's three co-equal officers who manage its affairs under the overall supervision of NCNB Corporation Chairman Thomas I. Storrs, Luther Hodges is, at 39, one of the major names in American banking.

There is speculation, which Mr. Hodges does not necessarily discourage, that in time he may embark upon the political highway in quest of a seat in the U.S. Senate or of the North Carolina Governor's Office. If that should happen, and if he should be successful, then the parallels between the career of Luther Hodges, Jr., and that of his late father would become even more striking.

One need not be cynical to question the degree to which the eminence of the elder Hodges as a leader in the textile industry, as Governor of North Carolina and as Secretary of Commerce might have aided the advancement of his son. To the younger Hodges, it is a fair and legitimate query, and one to which he responds with candor.

"There's no doubt that my father's being who he was opened some doors to me; I think that is true of almost any children of prominent parents," he said. "But then comes the reverse side of the coin. I believe there might be more pressure where the son has a famous father than might otherwise be the case. Such an individual may feel that he has to demonstrate an even higher level of performance in order to prove he isn't getting ahead because of his father's name."

Perhaps there are places of business where the holder of a highly-placed name might progress without conspicuous talent and capacity for work. Those who know the standards of North Carolina National Bank and its parent company say flatly that no one gets ahead in that organization, regardless of his name, on any other basis than that of performance.

NCNB's Hodges bears a physical resemblance to his father. His associates say he has the same reservoirs of energy and stamina. They are not as discernible in the younger Hodges — he doesn't speak as rapidly as did his father, nor does the father's remembered restlessness seem so close to the surface in the son.

But the activities of Luther, Jr. — for the bank and in the many unrelated public areas that are expected of him and to which his interest is naturally drawn — appear at least as extensive as those remembered of the Hodges who was Governor and a Cabinet officer. Luther, Jr., records the ten or eleven-hour office day which seems typical of high-ranking executives of large banks. His execu-

continued page 18

The North Carolina Citizens Association (now the North Carolina Chamber) presented me with a framed copy of the first page of a most complimentary article in their magazine about the new management team at NCNB. *Photo, left to right:* McColl, Dougherty, Hodges.

It was a strong group, with diverse but complementary personalities and talents. When he retired, Reese wrote that he was proud to turn over NCNB to the "best team in the banking business." But before his retirement, Reese was asked by some directors to recruit another vice chairman of NCNB Corporation in order to be certain that Tom Storrs was the correct successor. Tom Storrs had worked in Greensboro for several years in the early 1960s, and he was not particularly friendly with certain Greensboro directors. Hence, the company recruited Pete Taylor, a member of the management team of TransAmerica Insurance Corporation in San Francisco, to be a new vice chairman of NCNB Corporation. Taylor was California and not North Carolina, and he did not succeed in the Charlotte of those days.

The NCNB team was, for sure, young, ambitious, and determined to "beat the Wachovia Bank," which had been number one in the state since long before any of the team was born. And in 1972, NCNB surpassed Wachovia in banking assets and became the largest bank in the state and in the South. Beyond that, there was nowhere to go but across state lines. We felt that the South was the best region for banking, and McColl and I were less than impressed with the big-bank competition originating from New York and San Francisco.

Frankly, Hugh McColl and I were consumed by the possible opportunities of nationwide banking. We would dream and converse in my kitchen on Biltmore Drive in Charlotte in the mid-1960s about a new world of banking. We believed that the interstate barrier eventually had to fall, and when it did, a southern bank or two would grow to be among the largest in the country, and NCNB would be one of them.

One would assume that the largest bank in North Carolina and the South, Wachovia Bank and Trust Company, would dominate the southern scene, and such was the case for many years.

But what happened? According to Rick Rothacker's 2010 book *Banktown*, John Medlin (interestingly, a college mate of Hugh McColl's and mine), who became Wachovia CEO in 1977, was never concerned about the competition, because he felt that NCNB and First Union were overreaching and "on the edge." He was correct in that we were more aggressive, and the mid-1970s were difficult for all banking institutions in the Southeast. But Wachovia was simply more conservative and had always been, and conservatism in banking was not in vogue in the 1970s and 1980s. Moreover, I believe that some of my early observations about Wachovia's internal conformity and tight central control were accurate and were part of the reason the institution lost its position as the region's largest bank. Incidentally, when John Watlington retired in 1976, he had been president and CEO of Wachovia for some twenty years. I do not think anyone should be CEO of anything for that many years. In any event, First Union Bank eventually acquired Wachovia Bank, and Charlotte became home to two of the largest banks in the country.

CROSSING STATE LINES

Most bank holding companies operated with sizable levels of debt, and the recession of 1974 was a serious threat to NCNB Corporation and many of its competitors. To shore up banking relationships and lines of credit, Tom Storrs divided his management team into groups of two, with Dougherty and Storrs traveling to some major banks and Hodges and McColl taking responsibility for the remainder. Fortunately, this strategy was successful.

Some history is in order to properly appreciate the strategy for NCNB Corporation's success in moving outside of North Carolina following a full recovery from the recession of 1974. In 1971 the head of the Pittsburgh National Bank acquired, through its holding company, the Trust Company of Florida, a small institution outside of Orlando designed to keep the trust business of existing, wealthy customers as they retired to Florida. The Florida institution was not considered to be engaged in interstate banking, as it was a trust company and did not offer deposit accounts. Nevertheless, this Pittsburgh banker's board of directors almost immediately asked the president to sell the new subsidiary. Addison Reese, at his summer home in Nantucket, learned of the opportunity, and he, fortunately, was well acquainted with the CEO of Pittsburgh National Bank, who also vacationed on Nantucket Island. As a result, one of my responsibilities from 1974 until my resignation from NCNB was supervision of the Trust Company of Florida.

During the 1974 recession, Tom Storrs asked me to find a buyer and sell our Florida asset. I did not think that his request was a good idea for the bank's future, and I quietly ignored him. The facts surrounding this episode certainly were not revealed in the biography of NationsBank, written by Marion Ellis and Howard Covington. The authors were good, but they were under

The second NCNB building was completed in 1974.

the direction of the public relations office of NationsBank and of course reflected Tom Storrs' version of the events of 1974.

I cannot claim any sort of dramatic foresight to explain my inaction on Florida, but in 1981, NCNB Corporation used the Trust Company of Florida as a toehold in that state to slip through a loophole in Florida law and move into the lucrative Florida bank market. NCNB Corporation, through its Florida Trust Company, acquired First National Bank of Lake City, Gulf-stream Bank of Boca Raton, and the Ellis Banks of Bradenton. Eventually it would acquire the Barnett Bank, the largest bank in Florida. Those Florida acquisitions were the beginning of interstate banking, even though no laws had been changed to permit such expansion.

My decision not to sell the Trust Company of Florida was largely based on the fact that I thought NCNB Corporation was overreacting to the liquidity problems associated with the 1974 real estate recession. In fact, Tom Storrs, about to become CEO of NCNB Corporation, was scared to death of the company's liquidity problems, and he thus made some poor decisions. My decision in that year was that I no longer wanted to work for Tom Storrs, and I thought that I just might take my father's advice; namely, "once you have succeeded in the private sector, give yourself to the public sector." If a political life was in front of me, I certainly could not resign my position at the bank prior to the bank's return to operating success.

Other conversations with Tom Storrs in 1974 reflected his desire for me to avoid any loan commitments that might prove difficult for NCNB during the recession. The most problematic of these conversations was his request that we back out of my commitment to C. D. Spangler and his troubled Bank of North Carolina, headquartered in Jacksonville, N.C. I had promised a loan of $10 million to solve Dick Spangler's problems with the

Office of the Comptroller of the Currency. My inaction on this particular directive from Tom Storrs paved the way for Spangler to become the bank's largest shareholder (and easily one of North Carolina's wealthiest individuals) when his then-successful bank was merged into NationsBank in 1982. I was also asked to "call the loan" I had made to the new owner of our insurance agency, which I had been told to sell not too long before. I also ignored this order and knew that I would leave the bank at the first opportunity.

Frankly, as I reflect on taking my father's advice, I realize that I had probably succeeded in banking too quickly. With the exception of Tom Storrs, every officer to whom I had reported, and from whom I learned the business, ultimately worked for me. In any event, in 1977, after the bank and holding company had returned to profitability, I changed lives and ran for the Democratic nomination to the United States Senate, hoping to challenge Republican Jesse Helms in his first bid for reelection in the following year. I ran well ahead of a large field in the first round of the primary but was upset in the second round, or runoff.

I left the bank and lived outside the state for more than two decades, but I continued to watch and marvel at the ascension of NCNB. After NCNB was settled in Florida, political pressure was directed at the legislatures in many Southern states, and banking laws were subsequently altered so that branch banking was permitted among the states in the region. In 1983 the bank became NationsBank following its acquisition of the C&S National Bank in Atlanta, and ultimately NationsBank acquired Bank of America.

A Sabbatical with President Jimmy Carter

After my defeat at the polls in 1978, I had no intention of ever returning to the banking business. I did, however, think that meaningful public service existed at the Federal Reserve Bank in Washington. Such a position appealed to me, and a number of banking friends and supporters urged me to ask President Carter for an appointment to the Board of Governors of the Federal Reserve. Indeed, many bankers felt that the Fed needed someone more familiar with commercial banking on its twelve-person Board of Governors. Most appointees had come to Washington as professional economists or academicians.

My most active supporter was Bert Lance, a former banker from Georgia who was then the president's Director of the Office of Management and Budget. Bert Lance wrote a nice, personal note to his close friend on my behalf; however, Jimmy Carter had decided that his first appointment to the Fed's Board of Governors would be an African American or a woman. Coincidentally, the appointment in 1979 was Emmett Rice, a senior vice president and economist at The National Bank of Washington, which would be my new banking home throughout the 1980s.

In the spring of 1979, I was appointed undersecretary of commerce, in which position I worked for Juanita Kreps, a former professor of economics at Duke University and a friend whom I had invited a few years earlier to serve on the Board of Directors of North Carolina National Bank. Secretary Kreps, who had been an active supporter of mine for the position at the Federal Reserve, did not, because of her husband's serious illness, stay in Washington very long after my appointment. I assumed her duties, as acting secretary of commerce, for the remainder of 1979. I had little contact with the banking industry other than making speeches to various banking organizations, particularly

Luther H. Hodges Jr. is slated to be the new undersecretary of the U.S. Commerce Department.

Photograph from a June 2, 1979 article in *The Charlotte News*, titled "Commerce post waiting: Hodges is learning government ins, outs."

in the area of international banking. The greatest contribution made at the Department of Commerce in the Carter years was the creation of an undersecretary for foreign trade and a great expansion of the department's role in promoting exports from the United States. With the creation of additional undersecretaries, I was named the department's first deputy secretary.

WASHINGTON BANCORPORATION

1986 ANNUAL REPORT

*The National Bank of Washington
is the oldest bank in the Nation's Capital.
Founded in 1809, NBW financed the Washington Monument,
helped rebuild the city after the War of 1812, and
has served as the bank of Presidents
and pioneers throughout its history.*

*Today, NBW is the third largest bank
in the District of Columbia and the largest subsidiary
of Washington Bancorporation, a $1.8 billion
financial services corporation.*

*Washington Bancorporation is proud
to be located in the District of Columbia
and to serve as the "hometown bank"
for the Nation's Capital.*

**BY THE TIME THEY STARTED BUILDING
THE WASHINGTON MONUMENT,
WE'D BEEN HELPING BUILD WASHINGTON
FOR ALMOST 40 YEARS.**

It took an innovative bank to see the importance of helping to finance the
Washington Monument. And our tradition of leadership continues today.

 **THE NATIONAL BANK
OF WASHINGTON**

Washington's oldest bank. Founded 1809.   Member FDIC

Cover photography: Dick Swanson

THE NATIONAL BANK OF WASHINGTON

Immediately following the election in November 1980, I joined The National Bank of Washington (NBW) as its chairman of the board and chief executive officer. Early in his campaign for reelection, I had been told by President Carter that "he had North Carolina" and that he needed to reach out to another state for his appointment of a new secretary of commerce. I had been the deputy secretary and acting secretary for many months, and I had been promised the full title in the "second Carter Administration." Not believing that the president would be reelected, I immediately began talking to recruiting firms concerning opportunities back in commercial banking, and I ultimately chose the offer from The National Bank of Washington. Incidentally, President Carter did not carry North Carolina in the fall of 1980.

When I was considering the opportunity at NBW, I learned that the bank was considered a "problem institution" by its regulator, the Office of the Comptroller of the Currency (OCC). Indeed, the bank's future as an independent institution was considered quite questionable. The bank, the third-oldest in the United States, was 70 percent owned and fully controlled by the United Mine Workers of America (UMW).

Following World War II, the miners' union was a very strong institution, and its leader, John L. Lewis, was well known in Washington, D.C. Apparently, Mr. Lewis had become a good friend of James M. Johnston, ironically a native of North Carolina, who was a founder and managing director of Johnston Lemon & Company, a major local brokerage firm. Mr. Johnston convinced his friend to buy some of NBW's stock, and, as Lewis and his UMW were actively trying to enhance the union's position in the coal business, Lewis thought that owning a bank

National Bank: Hodges Sees A New Era

By BART FRAUST

NEW YORK — The National Bank of Washington, the largest of five union-owned commercial banks in the U.S., is lush with history — most of it good but some of it decidedly forgettable.

Originally incorporated in Maryland in 1809, the bank's customers have included James Madison, Henry Clay, Daniel Webster, Francis Scott Key, and Eli Whitney. The bank participated in the financing for construction of the Washington Monument.

LUTHER H. HODGES JR.

In the 1970s, though, National Bank of Washington was rocked by scandal, largely related to its association with the United Mine Workers of America.

The sale of the UMW ownership in NBW was widely covered by the press. Excerpt from *American Banker*, March 4, 1985.

and lending to customers in the coal industry would help him in unionizing more mining companies. The UMW ownership position increased over the years, and the union fully controlled the bank through its officers and friends who were appointed to the NBW board of directors. The union ultimately abused its fiduciary responsibilities by excessive lending to its friends, and by 1979, after many bad loans, the bank was taken over by the OCC.

In essence, the bank failed "the old-fashioned way." Today when a bank fails, the government, in the name of the Federal Deposit Insurance Corporation, takes over the institution and immediately sells it to another bank. In the old days, the government assumed full responsibility for managing the failed bank and nursing it back to good health. Accordingly, the government ordered the UMW to hire new management who had to be approved by the OCC.

At the time, I was a recognized banker and a Democrat, which presumably was more acceptable to the labor union. I also knew the then comptroller of the currency, John Heineman of New York, with whom I visited while considering the union's job offer. In any event, I was given the job, a reasonable contract, and a difficult challenge.

POWERBROKERS

Hodges emerges as District's most influential banking voice

By Christine Tierney

A relative newcomer to the area, his name has now become synonymous with banking in Washington. Luther Hodges, chairman of National Bank of Washington, the city's third largest bank, most recently made headlines when he engineered the purchase of the bank by a New York-based investment group, Colson Inc., from the bank's long-time owners, the United Mine Workers.

The sale was first announced in February. Then, at last month's shareholder meeting, Hodges revealed the identities of some members of the group, which includes many local heavyweights and two Manhattan-based institutional investors. He said Colson Inc. would meet the $70 million price named
continued on page 21A

Excerpt from *Washington Business Journal*, May 20, 1985.

I hired new bank officers, appointed new directors, and cleared all major decisions with the Richmond, Virginia, regional office of the OCC. Indeed, I traveled to Richmond at least monthly for several years. In 1985 the OCC released the bank from its supervision, and the following year, the labor union, which no longer controlled the bank but which had been permitted to keep its ownership in the institution, was paid $75 million for its stock holdings. To this day, no representative of the United Mine Workers of America has ever said "thank you" or "well done." In 1980 the union's investment was valued at zero!

As the bank grew and returned to profitability, the directors and I wanted to purchase the UMW's ownership, and in 1986 we were able to raise $100 million in additional capital. However, some 30 percent of that new money was provided by a Saudi Arabian businessman, who, at the time, was the world's largest arms merchant. In retrospect, I was naïve, for as the bank succeeded, my large shareholder did not want to raise capital from new investors. Rather, he wanted to own more of the bank and to block any sale of the institution. A strong majority of the board of directors and I ignored our Saudi Arabian partner and his representatives, and we attempted to raise capital through a well-known national brokerage firm in New York. A serious lawsuit followed, and we fought for two years, at which point, as a means of ending the costly court battle, I volunteered to resign if I was not able to sell the bank by the end of 1989. The climate for banking in 1989 was not good, and I was unable to sell NBW to a major international bank, as I had anticipated.

This announcement is neither an offer to sell nor a solicitation of an offer to buy these securities. The offer is made only by the Prospectus.

NEW ISSUE   October 7, 1987

700,000 Shares

WASHINGTON BANCORPORATION

Common Stock
$2.50 Par Value

Price: $17.875 Per Share

Copies of the Prospectus may be obtained from the undersigned only in States where the undersigned may legally offer these securities in compliance with the securities laws thereof.

KEEFE, BRUYETTE & WOODS, INC.

The proposed attempt to raise additional capital through New York's prestigious Keefe, Bruyette & Woods was thwarted by the Saudi Arabian investors, resulting in a bitter, expensive lawsuit.

619 Fourteenth Street, NW
Washington, DC 20005

Telephone
202 624 3010

Luther H. Hodges, Jr.
Chairman of the Board and
Chief Executive Officer

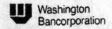
Washington
Bancorporation

January 26, 1990

Board of Directors
Washington Bancorporation and
The National Bank of Washington

Gentlemen:

Consistent with the terms of the Settlement Agreement among
the directors of Washington Bancorporation, The National Bank
of Washington, and the principal shareholder of Washington
Bancorporation, I hereby submit my resignation as Chairman of
the Board of Directors and as a director of Washington
Bancorporation and The National Bank of Washington, as of
January 31, 1990.

At the time the Settlement Agreement was negotiated some ten
months ago, I had identified a purchaser for the stock of the
principal shareholder, and today I have such an investor;
however, subsequent events demanded that a buyer for 100% of
the shares of Washington Bancorporation be identified. The
banking environment in 1989, plus certain conditions unique
to The National Bank of Washington, including continued
litigation, have precluded such a sale on the terms
identified in the Settlement Agreement. An independent,
special committee of the Board of Directors of Washington
Bancorporation continues to work with your investment
bankers.

I am proud of the dramatic progress that has been achieved at
this company since the low point of The National Bank of
Washington ten years ago. A very professional management
team and many, many able employees have served you well under
very challenging circumstances. I am forever grateful for
the personal loyalty of the great majority of our directors,
but I deplore the damage that has been done to a great
institution because of 28 months of uncertainty, turmoil, and
hostility within our boards of directors.

Luther H. Hodges, Jr.

619 Fourteenth Street, NW
Washington, DC 20005

Telephone
202 624 3010

Luther H. Hodges, Jr.
Chairman of the Board and
Chief Executive Officer

The National Bank
of Washington

January 29, 1990

WBC Associates,

As you have probably heard by now, I have submitted the attached
letter to the Board of Directors. I believe the Board will move
quickly to appoint a new Chairman and our company should be able
to return to activities that more properly deserve our full
attention -- providing the best banking services in the Nation's
Capital.

In our 180 year history, the bank has weathered many storms. I
believe we will emerge from this one standing tall and proud.

I regret that I will not be with you to finish what we started
together, but I appreciate your loyalty and support. I applaud
your diligent efforts throughout this period of uncertainty. And,
when you accomplish what this great institution is capable of, I
will take special pride in your success.

I look forward to visiting with you personally in the near future.
In the meantime, never let the bastards see you sweat!

Sincerely,

Luther H. Hodges, Jr.

Reflections on Bank Regulation
and the Future of Banking

I focus on the failure of NBW not for any personal reason, but because today we hear comments to the effect that even in the face of the ineffective Dodd-Frank legislation of 2010, we need more bank regulation. Actually, NBW was awarded a satisfactory rating by its regulator, the U.S. Office of the Comptroller of the Currency, just prior to my resignation in 1989.

The routine bank examination of NBW in November 1989 revealed a "CAMEL rating" that was actually positive. The examination focused on the bank's capital adequacy; that is to say, C, its level of capital; A, its asset quality, following a complete review of the loan portfolio and its "Allowance for Possible Loan Losses;" M, the abilities of the bank's management; E, the bank's earnings and profitability; and L, the bank's liquidity, or ability to contend with any financial crisis. This bank, which enjoyed a CAMEL rating of "satisfactory" at a time when there was virtually no higher rating, failed within six months of my departure. Frankly, banks in 1990 and before were considered, along with electric utilities, to be the most regulated sector of the U.S. economy. What was needed was better regulators and a more practical, efficient regulatory environment, not more regulation. Such are the circumstances today.

When I resigned from NBW, the lawsuit was not settled as promised, and as soon as the bank failed in the summer of 1990, the U.S. government assumed the plaintiff's role in the lawsuit against me and a majority of the individual bank directors. Little did anyone in Washington know that the Saudi Arabian investor in NBW was exceptionally close to the Saudi Arabian ambassador, Prince Bandar, and the ambassador's father, the Saudi Arabian defense minister. Nor did we realize the leverage that my investor had with the U.S. government because of the military alliance with which we are now quite familiar: Desert Storm, the war with Iraq that followed Saddam Hussein's invasion of Kuwait, waged from modern military bases in Saudi Arabia.

Years later, after more than $1 million in personal legal fees, the government's lawsuit over the failure of The National Bank of Washington was dismissed by a federal judge "with criticism of the government's role." I endeavored to write a book about this entire matter but was told by book editors and publishers that there had already been too many publications about "the financial excesses of the 1980s." My response was that my book would not be about the mistakes of the banking industry; rather, I wanted to write about the failure of bank regulation and bank regulators. Actually, NBW is a very good example of poor regulation, because the government violated its own rules for bank ownership in permitting the Saudi Arabian investment in the Washington bank. Similarly, the federal government was blind to the secret takeover of Washington's First American National Bank by the Pakistani Bank of Commerce and Credit International (BCCI).

NBW was not alone with its problems with the Office of the Comptroller of the Currency. Many banks failed in the late 1980s. Indeed, the nation had suffered a serious real estate crisis, one that completely wiped out traditional savings and loan associations. Moreover, the price of oil declined along with most real estate values, and in Texas, nine of the ten largest banks failed. Ironically, the Texas problem was compounded by its state law prohibiting branch banking. The Texas bankers finally convinced the state's legislature to alter its traditional laws concerning bank branching, but such efforts were much too late. The most notable failure was that of First Republic National Bank in Dallas, which NCNB had acquired from the

Currently
the Charlotte
headquarters
of the Bank
of America,
affectionally
known as the
Taj McColl.

Federal Deposit Insurance Corporation in 1988, a truly major development in the growth of NationsBank. I found this acquisition in particular to be an extraordinary indicator of the changing times, as Hugh McColl and I had been in Dallas in 1974 pleading with the then Republic National Bank to continue its $10 million line of credit to NCNB Corporation.

As banking and the economy improved in the 1990s, the pressure to permit interstate banking increased. Indeed, Hugh McColl and his good friend, Erskine Bowles, were able to encourage President Clinton to support legislation for interstate banking. We will never know of the conversations among McColl, Bowles, and Clinton, but we do know that Crandall Bowles and then First Lady Hillary Clinton had been classmates at Wellesley College. Moreover, Bowles, a very knowledgeable investment banker from North Carolina, spent part of his time in the Clinton administration as the President's chief of staff.

NationsBank aggressively capitalized on the new banking laws, particularly with its acquisition in 1999 of the Boatman's National Bank in St Louis. Subsequently, rumors suggested that a "merger of equals" would take place between NationsBank and the Bank of America of San Francisco. That scenario had the new Bank of America headquartered in Washington or Chicago, but that transaction was never consummated. However, as the Bank of America's troubles mounted, McColl and NationsBank waited, and finally the California bank was acquired on McColl's terms. Charlotte became the headquarters of the new Bank of America.

Meanwhile, in North Carolina, both First Union Corporation and Wachovia Corporation enjoyed their own acquisitions and much internal growth. One surprising acquisition ultimately saw First Union buying the legendary Wachovia Bank, and that transaction resulted in First Union's taking the more famous name of Wachovia, just as NationsBank had assumed the name Bank of America. Charlotte thus became the headquarters of two of the largest banks in the world, and from afar I proudly congratulated Hugh McColl and his team for such dramatic success in the new banking environment.

I find it interesting to reflect on the late 1960s, when NCNB joined a handful of important banks to license BankAmericard from the famous California bank. That successful credit card franchise soon became Visa. Competing banks, such as Wachovia Bank and Trust Company in North Carolina, formed another company, MasterCard, in order to capitalize on the great trend for banks to provide full credit card services. Today, people talk of a new day in banking when technology will soon permit instant consumer purchases without the need for credit cards.

The Great Financial Recession

By 2007 all large banks were in serious trouble, and the federal government began encouraging mergers and acquisitions to save troubled banks. Poor underwriting of home loans and the failure of the mortgage banks, which had been acquired over the previous decade, created a disaster. Wachovia, particularly, was hit by the problems at its subsidiary, Golden West Financial Corporation, resulting in the government forcing the sale of Wachovia to Wells Fargo Bank in San Francisco. Bank of America, while remaining alive and independent, suffered greatly from its acquisition of CountryWide Financial, at the time the largest mortgage banking firm in the country. Moreover, in the following year the Bank of America, with much encouragement from the federal government, acquired the major investment banking company Merrill, Lynch.

Without delving into the complex details of the "great recession," I must advance the rather obvious point that commercial banking, since the many bank failures of 2008, has changed dramatically. In my opinion, much of the blame lies with the federal government, not the bankers. I recognize that most people blame the recession on "Wall Street and the bankers." And blame may be on both sides, for surely there are bad bankers, but there also are bad preachers, bad teachers, bad doctors, bad bank regulators, and bad Indian chiefs!

Although many Americans and many in Congress assumed that the banks made the bad mortgage loans that sank the economy, in fact our federal government had been encouraging lower underwriting standards for home mortgages for at least thirty years. In the 1970s and '80s, when I was a very active banker, if a bank applied to the Federal Reserve for permission to merge or to enter a new financial business, ACORN, the Association of Community Organizations for Reform Now, would threaten to file a lawsuit if the targeted bank did not agree to modify its credit standards for residential mortgages, particularly in specific, minority neighborhoods.

As time passed, Presidents Clinton and George W. Bush set high percentages of homeownership as major policy goals of the federal government. Moreover, government-backed "housing agencies," Fannie Mae and Freddie Mac, insured the mortgages being written, thus presumably removing any risk to the banks for the lower standards for home mortgages. Additionally, the three major credit rating agencies—Moody's, Standard & Poor's, and Fitch—all gave securities, which were home mortgages packaged and sold by the bad bankers, a most positive credit rating, typically Triple A. No questions were ever raised by the government during this period, and I will never understand how banks are today accused of fraud, yet little is said about the rating agencies. Similarly, in international banking, governments gave high ratings to bank loans to any foreign country, including Greece!

As the mortgage loans were sold into the market, the true quality of the poorly underwritten mortgages was revealed, as homeowners began to default on the loans. Not only did many banks fail because of defaulting home loans, but the nation also witnessed the failure of the government's housing agencies, Fannie Mae and Freddie Mac. In 2008, these "quasi-government agencies" were placed into government conservatorship, with taxpayers footing the bill for a $188 billion bailout. Meanwhile, the Federal Reserve Bank maintained the cost of money at an inordinately low level of interest rates for over a decade. In essence, the government was very much responsible for the great financial recession.

RETHINKING THE BANKING BUSINESS

Looking to the future, many feel that our government had erred in the 1990s by amending the Glass-Steagall Act of 1933, thus permitting interstate banking and abolishing the "wall" between commercial and investment banking that had been created during the Great Depression. When, in 1966, Hugh McColl and I used to talk about the future of banking, we certainly foresaw interstate banking, but we also thought in terms of banks' becoming financial department stores and bankers acting more as financial consultants. The financial department store would offer one-stop shopping for all of a customer's needs in the area of financial services. Thus, investment banking and the brokerage business were a part of that dream.

Unfortunately the banking industry and its leaders, during a period of rapid innovation and unprecedented growth at the turn of the last century, could not cope with the significant problems (subprime loans, collateralized debt obligations, and credit default swaps) created by the new mortgage companies which commercial and investment banks had acquired. While I still believe in the financial department store concept, I tend to agree with former Federal Reserve Chairman Paul Volcker, who has argued that commercial bank holding companies should not be permitted to invest their own funds in the securities markets.

Additionally, the Dodd-Frank Law of 2010, named for Senator Chris Dodd of Connecticut and Representative Barney Frank of Massachusetts, has been a disaster and, indeed, the cause of many current problems associated with the excessive regulation of banking. The legislation was based on the premise that the "great recession" was the result of the previous decade's deregulation of banking. Both legislators, true populists, believed that bankers, certainly not the government, were the cause of the financial crisis, and that new, stronger regulations were needed. The simple facts are that regulatory restrictions on banks grew every year between 1999 and 2008, and, just as with the failure of The National Bank of Washington, the real problem was poor, uncoordinated, arguably excessive regulation, not deregulation.

Today regulators are making new laws and involving themselves in the active management of banks, and clearly the Federal Reserve Bank is making monetary policy while regulating, and virtually managing, our banking system. To quote the *Wall Street Journal* of December 3, 2015, "relentless pressure from regulators is forcing banking to do business differently in the wake of the financial crisis." For example, the legislation designed to thwart the practice of "money laundering" requires bankers to virtually testify that they know the source of any large deposit by a customer and that the deposit, or related payment flows, are in the normal course of that customer's business.

The new regulations seem to have made banking far more difficult for both the banker and the customer, with the result that the customer begins to look at non-regulated organizations for borrowing money. And today's new technology is also leading to further weakening of traditional banking as, for example, smart phones replacing credit cards. Another illustration of banks' retreating from their traditional business model is the decline in large corporate loans. Today new entities make such loans, resulting in a shift of assets to hedge funds and new areas of the financial sector that are outside of the purview of the regulators. We are, in essence, promoting a new "shadow banking system" that benefits very few citizens.

Another great casualty of current overregulation, including the Dodd-Frank legislation, is today's lack of new business activity and the related dearth of new jobs. We teach and promote entrepreneurship, but overregulation discourages new businesses. Small businesses, including small banks, have seen costs rise dramatically with the result of little or no growth in employment. While small banks have traditionally been most helpful to small businesses, the rate of new bank formations has dropped from an average of hundred a year prior to 2010 to only three per year currently.

Accompanying our poor bank regulatory system, our government made the great mistake in 2008 of not permitting the market to correct itself. Commercial banks and investment banks have failed in the past with no serious macroeconomic consequences. Accordingly, our government's response in 2008 should have been to let both investment banks Bear Stearns and Lehman Brothers fail, as opposed to confusing the market by supporting one and not the other.

In essence, the decisions made by the government during the fall of 2008 sent conflicting messages to the market and brought the government fully into the management of the banking business. I believe that the system would have corrected itself. Moreover, I do not think that any institution should be considered too big to fail.

The illegibility of this illustration of the many rules applicable to U.S. Financial Services Holding Companies should convince any reader that today's banks are overregulated.

Original illustration released to the public by SEC Commissioner Daniel M. Gallagher on March 2, 2015. Full size image available for download at https://www.sec.gov/news/statement/aggregate-impact-of-financial-services-regulation.html

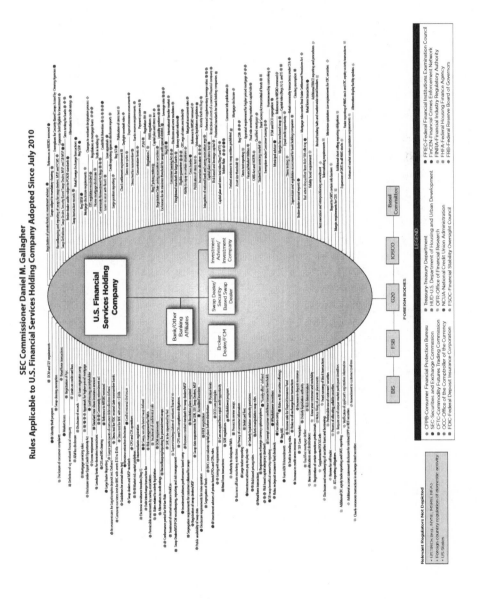

This 2010 chart illustrates the fact that, over just 20 years, 37 banks have merged to become "The Big Four."

Reprinted with permission from *Mother Jones*, "How Banks Got Too Big to Fail."

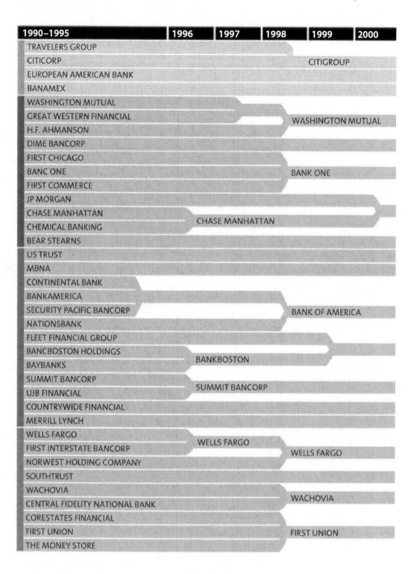

1990–1995	1996	1997	1998	1999	2000
TRAVELERS GROUP					
CITICORP				CITIGROUP	
EUROPEAN AMERICAN BANK					
BANAMEX					
WASHINGTON MUTUAL					
GREAT WESTERN FINANCIAL				WASHINGTON MUTUAL	
H.F. AHMANSON					
DIME BANCORP					
FIRST CHICAGO					
BANC ONE				BANK ONE	
FIRST COMMERCE					
JP MORGAN					
CHASE MANHATTAN		CHASE MANHATTAN			
CHEMICAL BANKING					
BEAR STEARNS					
US TRUST					
MBNA					
CONTINENTAL BANK					
BANKAMERICA					
SECURITY PACIFIC BANCORP				BANK OF AMERICA	
NATIONSBANK					
FLEET FINANCIAL GROUP					
BANCBOSTON HOLDINGS		BANKBOSTON			
BAYBANKS					
SUMMIT BANCORP		SUMMIT BANCORP			
UJB FINANCIAL					
COUNTRYWIDE FINANCIAL					
MERRILL LYNCH					
WELLS FARGO		WELLS FARGO			
FIRST INTERSTATE BANCORP				WELLS FARGO	
NORWEST HOLDING COMPANY					
SOUTHTRUST					
WACHOVIA				WACHOVIA	
CENTRAL FIDELITY NATIONAL BANK					
CORESTATES FINANCIAL					
FIRST UNION				FIRST UNION	
THE MONEY STORE					

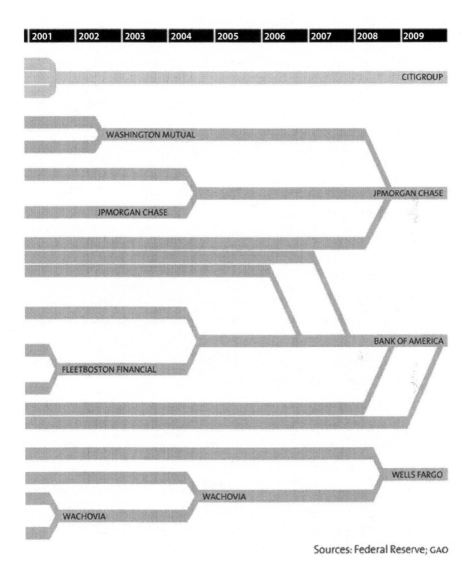

| 2001 | 2002 | 2003 | 2004 | 2005 | 2006 | 2007 | 2008 | 2009 |

CITIGROUP

WASHINGTON MUTUAL

JPMORGAN CHASE

JPMORGAN CHASE

FLEETBOSTON FINANCIAL

BANK OF AMERICA

WELLS FARGO

WACHOVIA

WACHOVIA

Sources: Federal Reserve; GAO

Comments on the Future of Banking

Today we have a far different banking environment than when Hugh McColl and I dreamed of, and planned for, "the bank for all of America." In those early days, there were some twenty thousand banks in the United States, along with some twenty thousand savings and loan associations. Our economy had too many such institutions; banking was clearly inefficient. Today, we have no savings and loan associations, and only some six thousand banks, with the vast majority of bank deposits concentrated in a handful of institutions. Incidentally, it is easier today to charter a new bank in the United Kingdom than it is to open a new bank in the United States. Moreover, in Great Britain, as well as all major developed counties, the number of banks is a minute fraction of those in the United States.

When the ambitious young bankers at the North Carolina National Bank were planning for interstate banking, we knew that our banking system had to change. Change certainly occurred, but strong, growing, and profitable banks, which are critical to our economic future, are no longer a central part of our economy. What do we do?

First, enough time has passed since the financial crisis of 2008 so that we should be able to identify and agree on the causes of the problem, and, if humanly possible, we need to intellectually, not politically, improve our banking system. Improvement involves more equity on the banks' balance sheets. I am certain that today's bankers would accept the increased cost associated with less leverage if they could be free of expensive new regulation and of the requirement for many employees in compliance departments dedicated to virtually working for the government.

Secondly, unless someone wants to nationalize all banks, we

must reduce the overall regulatory environment that has proven expensive and frequently irrelevant. A review of SEC Commissioner Daniel M. Gallagher's illustration of "Rules Applicable to U.S. Financial Services Holding Companies" should convince any reader that today's banks are overregulated. These regulations are directed at those institutions deemed too big to fail. Smaller regional banks would be well advised, in today's environment, to stay below the designated threshold of heavy regulation.

Many observers of banking at this time might argue that we truly need a regulatory state to offset the law of the jungle. The "jungle," incidentally, is simply open competition, and the fear that some people associate with a free market. But the jungle of capitalism has given our country an exceptional economy and a world of opportunity.

We should not mortgage our economic future by permitting countless new regulations that are irrationally advanced in order to avoid future "banking crises." These new laws are enacted without a clear vision of the future of banking or of the impact of the laws. Plus we have innumerable regulatory agencies frequently competing with each other. For example, we have some five major federal regulatory agencies for national banking associations, and each federal regulator, and some members of Congress, are playing for political attention with laws that they represent will protect our citizens from banking excesses. Actually little coordination exists, and no one addresses the possible negative consequences of the many new laws and regulations.

A current debate involves the chairman of the Federal Deposit Insurance Corporation questioning the rationale for a new regulation from the Board of Governors of the Federal Reserve System. The Fed now seeks more debt on a bank's balance sheet as a "total loss-absorbing capacity" to prevent future bank bailouts. The FDIC sees such requirements as bad policy for smaller banking institutions. Clearly, one size does not fit all. Additionally, the Securities and Exchange Commission is today considering "standards for bank investments." Surely, no one thinks that investment risk can be controlled by regulation!

Lastly, our government has sued, settled, and fined many banks for an estimated $180 billion since 2008. Few private institutions can afford to fight the U.S. government in court, but for political reasons, the government has to show that someone has been guilty of hurting our economy. We have had countless settlements with banks over alleged liability, and we constantly talk about the "bad bankers," but we have not legally found any institutions or individuals guilty of criminal intent.

I do not believe that you can legislate ethics, but I do believe that ethics is an enormously important subject. Indeed, all employees of banks and financial institutions should be required by their employer to always act in the best interest of the depositor or customer. Good ethics should be part of the corporate culture within the banks (and, indeed, all businesses), and senior management should ensure that the culture is obvious to all employees.

In essence, our banks should be managed by their boards of directors and their chosen executives, and bank employees should be held to an especially high standard of conduct. Banks must be totally transparent in their operations, and we should want them to grow and prosper. We can appreciate the largest banks just as many respect Wal-Mart Stores (even as the giant retailer moves into the banking business). And those depositors who deplore bigness can comfortably utilize our many smaller, regional banks, which serve their communities so very well.

The federal government should oversee our national economy

to protect investors, borrowers, and lenders from corrupt, predatory, or blatantly incompetent business practices. But risking failure for the chance to achieve success is the way our economy works, and for most Americans, most of the time, it has worked pretty well. Bank management should be free to manage the banks of the future. And the banks and their employees should be free to fail!

Appendix

Written immediately following my first banking job, I intended this letter detailing my impressions about the Wachovia culture to be helpful. I later learned that my candid insights were not appreciated.

ASHEVILLE   BURLINGTON   CHARLOTTE
DURHAM   GOLDSBORO   GREENSBORO

WACHOVIA
BANK AND TRUST COMPANY

HIGH POINT   LA GRANGE   RALEIGH
SALISBURY   WILMINGTON   WINSTON-SALEM

CHARLOTTE 1, N. C.

1 September 1960

Mr. George P. Geoghegan, Jr.
Regional Vice President
Wachovia Bank and Trust Company
Raleigh, North Carolina

Dear Mr. Geoghegan:

We have often threatened to have a visit during which I could reflect in general on my summer as a commercial banker and, more specifically, on the activities of the Charlotte office of Wachovia. First, let me note that I am most grateful to Wachovia for the opportunity I have had to view banking, and I would like for this letter to you to be some token of my appreciation and, at the same time, serve as a summary of my thoughts on the summer—a review that will admittedly be more beneficial to me, as I attempt to clarify my impressions.

As I once mentioned, I was initially assigned to the Credit Department for the summer. I believe this placement was considered due to the similarity of my association with cases at Harvard Business School and the study and reference of company case histories in that department. Also, as a phase of the general training program, the Credit Department entailed approximately a summer's duration and, further, I think Credit was considered to be the department from which I could best observe total banking operations. I enjoyed my apprenticeship in the Credit Department during which time I read extensively and attended all Loan Committee meetings. After approximately one month, however, I felt as though I had mastered as much of the actual administration of credit as was possible without my living with each account and, realizing that I would be leaving Charlotte and that, consequently, there was little I could do for each file, I became restless with my lack of productivity.

As the summer progressed, I was permitted the luxury of a free reign within most departments of the bank with the result that I spent one week with the Loan and Discount tellers, a lesser period with the collection teller, attended a Personnel Committee meeting, visited in the Audit Department for a few days, which included an audit of a branch bank, assisted in the Cashier's Section for a day, and observed all operational phases during a week's stay in that department. Further, I was privileged to travel with the Correspondent Bank Division on four trips with a view to the extension of credit through overlines and to Wachovia's general relationship with its correspondent banks and the related commercial and individual accounts located outside of Charlotte. In addition, I visited in a branch office and participated in the local call program.

Any training program presents the dilemma of how to acquaint a potential executive with each aspect of the bank's operations while affording him some specific task, some responsibility that satisfies his personal ambitions. The problem is also complicated by the degree of prior education or experience that the new employee brings to the bank. Certainly my situation was no exception.

I should confess that on occasion I have stated that had I known that I would work for Wachovia I would not have gone to graduate school, for I have often felt that my time could have best been spent with the bank or in this area familiarizing myself with local personalities and commercial activity. I am convinced, of course, of the benefits of my advanced education—the confidence and experience that I can absorb, but for the moment the time when my position in commercial banking will value these qualities seems far away, and I note that the training program permits a liberal arts graduate to learn of both basic banking and Wachovia while the man with both a liberal arts and a business degree spends the same period learning only of Wachovia.

I mentioned my desire to acquaint myself with individuals and their businesses, the need to live in one's banking area. I have found banking to be extremely personal—more of the "salesman" is required than I had anticipated, and, consequently, I feel that today's banker must be familiar with, and active in, his community. This attracts me, because I too want to serve my community, and, further, the idea that I can render some aid to a variety of businesses by diversifying my experience and interests appeals to me. In this regard, I am quite fond of the definition of a commercial banker as a "man with a modified ignorance in all trades."

Actually my only reservation about my summer's activity concerned the personal aspect of banking to which I have just referred. The individual customer is all important to a bank's relationship and that certain understanding that is reached between the bank and the borrowing customer is usually developed only through one member of the staff. I would have enjoyed observing this exchange—that is, seeing an actual credit request, following the conversation, and trying my hand at understanding, and knowing, the borrower. Since the character of the individual is the basis of any loan, this personal association would seem to me to be the post graduate session for any training program. I shall be the first to note, however, that the third man can inhibit any conversation, and my presence during a serious loan request would involve the complete acceptance of me by a loan officer. This does not occur in one summer.

Let me add to my brief comments on the training program. As the Charlotte office envisioned, the Credit Department was my best vantage point. But, as is often the criticism of a training program—namely, that assignments are vague and that the trainee is paid for little productive effort, I served mainly as an observer, and whatever contribution I could have made by virtue of my experience with financial case studies at Harvard Business School was lost. Whoever the trainee, I feel that he should be given a definite assignment, a specific loan application, and told to render some decision. Only in this manner can an individual's particular credit talents be developed. I believe that as credit training now exists the novice merely mirrors the thoughts and reactions of the existing credit officer. Fortunately, the Charlotte office is blessed with a Credit Manager who seems to me to be quite capable and who gives each application the appropriate, personal attention. Today the trainee reflects a good credit image, but the training itself is lacking.

If, at this time, I were to consider a department in the Charlotte office for my possible employment, I would heartily endorse the Correspondent Bank Division. I was fortunate enough to be able to make three overnight trips into South Carolina and one visit to a neighboring North Carolina county, so I do feel as though I am familiar with the duties and objectives of this phase of Wachovia's activity. I have found the nature of the accounts and the fellowship of the bankers and businessmen throughout this area to be both challenging and rewarding. I have observed that the correspondent banker by virtue of his association with all phases of banking is readily able to render a service to a particular organization and, further, that he can easily view the progress of any contribution that he, or his bank, is making.

Although I enjoy referring to Wachovia as the leading bank in the southeast, and while I am proud to travel throughout our entire area, I would like to see Wachovia in Charlotte devote more correspondent activity to its North Carolina area. The Charlotte office admittedly has done a marvelous job in cultivating the entire State of South Carolina for Wachovia and, though I am sure that this fine relationship will continue to prosper, it should not do so to the neglect of our friends—or potential friends—in the next county. For my information, I chose to make a rough comparison of the number of accounts—disregarding dollar balances, if that is possible—to the number of banks in North Carolina and South Carolina. I found that about 65 percent of all the banks in the State of South Carolina carry some balances with Wachovia; however, only 50 percent of the some 50 banks in the Charlotte office's 15 county area in North Carolina bank with Wachovia. If we were to consider the dollar contribution, I am sure the proportion would be even heavier for the out of state banks. I have often found myself cheering for South Carolina, and I would not like to see Wachovia lose a single South Carolina relationship; nevertheless, the Charlotte office should protect itself by having at least an equal number of friends in its North Carolina area.

As I once related to you, my initial interest in Wachovia lay with the inauguration of its International Department. This interest still exists even though I have found this new department to be truly foreign—literally and figuratively—to those in Charlotte. I have always felt that the bank would realize a great potential as it participated in the development of North

Carolina's ports and foreign trade. Certainly today, as more local firms are purchasing and distributing abroad, we can begin to divert native resources back to North Carolina. I realize that the Foreign Department is presently, of necessity, in the embryonic stage, but I am eager to observe its future development.

As I prepare to close, let me just refer to what, I am sure, is a major question in every Wachovia executive's mind—namely, the degree of centralization, or decentralization, that will best permit each office to prosper within the general framework of a growing Wachovia Bank and Trust Company. There are, of course, numerous advantages in permitting the local officers to administer their own houses, and, similarly, elements of control and conformity which demand central authority. I do not pretend to have an answer that satisfies both sides, but my view of the Credit Department in Charlotte, where numerous loans exceeding $100,000 come under heavy control, did indicate that the image of Winston-Salem frequently loomed too large in the administration of local affairs. Possibly I should avoid the subject of Winston-Salem versus Charlotte, for more thought than I could ever offer has determined the existing, comparatively decentralized system, and, further, I will be the first to acknowledge that criteria must be established and met for proper credit and administrative procedures. But I have viewed a problem, and I am now merely reflecting on this point so that I can more fully appreciate the situation. I certainly do not question the standards—only the idea that people must be afraid of them.

I shall stay with the centralization idea for one additional observation. Before I went to business school, I had little faith in any advertising. Now that I have been exposed to some selling techniques I have a great deal of respect for good advertising. Being in Charlotte, I have been able to observe further the differences between good, creative copy and just advertising. The

Charlotte office appears to be in a somewhat reversed competitive position from most other Wachovia offices, and I would think that an attempt at originality at the local level to meet competition would be most appropriate.

I could continue at some length to describe the virtues of Wachovia, but I shall conclude with the above comments, which, by their frankness, may prove to be of some interest to you. I have tried to be honest and objective. I do not want to be critical. I am indebted to Wachovia for my experience, and I only hope that my observations can serve as some witness to my continued interest in, and support of, Wachovia Bank and Trust Company.

Most sincerely,

Luther H. Hodges, Jr.

LHHJr/jn

CC: Mr. R. H. Tate
Senior Vice President
Wachovia Bank and Trust Company
Wilmington, North Carolina

This announcement is neither an offer to sell nor a solicitation of an offer to buy the securities. The offer is made only by the Prospectus

New Issue / February 22, 1974

$75,000,000

NCNB Corporation

8⅞% Sinking Fund Debentures, due 1999

Interest is payable September 1 and March 1

Price 99.75% and accrued interest, if any, from March 1, 1974

Copies of the Prospectus may be obtained in any State in which this announcement is circulated only from such of the undersigned as may legally offer these securities in such State.

Salomon Brothers

Morgan Stanley & Co. *Incorporated*	The First Boston Corporation	Dillon, Read & Co. Inc.
Donaldson, Lufkin & Jenrette *Securities Corporation*	Drexel Burnham & Co. *Incorporated*	Goldman, Sachs & Co.
Halsey, Stuart & Co. Inc. *Affiliate of Bache & Co. Incorporated*	Hornblower & Weeks-Hemphill, Noyes *Incorporated*	E. F. Hutton & Company Inc.
Keefe, Bruyette & Woods, Inc.	Kidder, Peabody & Co. *Incorporated*	Kuhn, Loeb & Co.
Lazard Frères & Co.	Lehman Brothers *Incorporated*	Loeb, Rhoades & Co.
Merrill Lynch, Pierce, Fenner & Smith *Incorporated*		Paine, Webber, Jackson & Curtis *Incorporated*
Reynolds Securities Inc.	M. A. Schapiro & Co., Inc.	Smith, Barney & Co. *Incorporated*
Stone & Webster Securities Corporation	Wertheim & Co., Inc.	White, Weld & Co. *Incorporated*
Dean Witter & Co. *Incorporated*	Robert Garrett & Sons, Inc.	Interstate Securities Corporation

A "one-bank holding company" allowed commercial banks to access the national capital markets in order to take advantage of growth opportunities in financial services.

NCNB Corporation Annual Report, 1973
Management Profiles

A number of senior management changes were effective January 1 of this year, after the retirement of Board Chairman Addison H. Reese at year end.

Following are brief biographies of each of the members of the new NCNB Corporation management team:

Thomas I. Storrs

Storrs, previously president of the corporation and the bank and chief executive officer of the bank, is chairman of the board of the corporation, chairman of the executive committee of the bank and chief executive officer of both.

He began his banking career in 1934 at the Federal Reserve Bank of Richmond, Va. After working there for three years, he went to the University of Virginia where he graduated with a bachelor of arts degree.

He returned to the Federal Reserve Bank as a statistical clerk, became an economist in 1945, was promoted to assistant vice president in 1952 and in 1956 became vice president in charge of research. He moved to Charlotte in 1959 as vice president in charge of the Federal Reserve branch. While with the Federal Reserve, he attended Harvard University for two years to complete work for a master's degree and a doctorate in economics. Storrs, 55, joined North Carolina National Bank in 1960 as executive vice president. He was named vice chairman in 1967, president of the holding company in 1968, president of the bank in 1969 and chief executive officer of the bank in January 1973.

WILLIAM H. DOUGHERTY JR.

Dougherty, who was vice chairman of the corporation, is president of the corporation.

He is a native of Liberty Borough, Pa., and an honor graduate of the University of Pittsburgh with a business administration degree in accounting. After serving two years in the U. S. Air Force, he worked from 1954 to 1959 with Price Waterhouse & Co. in Pittsburgh, during which time he became a certified public accountant. He joined Western Pennsylvania National Bank (now Equibank) in 1959 as vice president-finance and cashier. Dougherty, 43, joined North Carolina National Bank as senior vice president and management services excecutive. He assumed additional responsibilities in late 1967 when appointed management services and operations executive. In December 1968 he was named executive vice president and support group executive of the bank and executive vice president and chief financial officer of the corporation. He became vice chairman of the corporation in January 1973.

Luther H. Hodges Jr.

Hodges, who formerly was vice chairman of the bank, has become chairman of the board of the bank.

A native of Leaksville (now Eden), N. C., Hodges, 37, is a 1957 Phi Beta Kappa graduate of the University of North Carolina at Chapel Hill with a bachelor of arts degree in economics. He received a master's degree in business administration from the Harvard Graduate School of Business Administration in 1961.

After serving for a year on the faculty of the School of Business Administration at the University of North Carolina, Hodges joined North Carolina National Bank in 1962. He was named vice president in charge of the Eastern Area of the National Division in 1964, senior vice president and Chapel Hill city executive in 1967, Charlotte city executive in 1968, executive vice president in charge of all North Carolina banking offices in 1970 and vice chairman of the bank in January 1973.

Hugh L. McColl Jr.

McColl, former vice chairman of the bank, is now president of the bank.

A native of Bennettsville, S. C., he joined North Carolina National Bank in 1959. He earned a bachelor of science degree in business administration from the University of North Carolina at Chapel Hill.

McColl, 38, became a correspondent bank relations representative in 1960, assistant cashier in the Correspondent Department in 1961, vice president and area director for the National Division in 1965, senior vice president in 1968, National Division executive in 1969, executive vice president in charge of international, national and correspondent banking in 1970 and vice chairman of the bank in January 1973.

Dougherty, Hodges and McColl, who were elected to the NCNB Corporation Board of Directors in April 1972 and to the bank's board in January 1973, report to Storrs.

Commerce post waiting

Hodges is learning government ins, outs

By WHITNEY SHAW
News Business Editor

Luther H. Hodges Jr. sat in a VIP lounge off the lobby of Charlotte's Radisson Plaza Hotel and — for just a brief moment — held his head in his hands.

Seconds before, Hodges had been told that a federal judge had declared a key part of President Carter's anti-inflation guidelines unconstitutional.

Not long ago, he would have been simply an interested observer. Now he is a participant.

For the past couple of months, the former chairman of the board of Charlotte's North Carolina National Bank has been working as a consultant to the Carter administration.

He will become Undersecretary of the United States Department of Commerce as soon as the Senate approves his nomination.

"I can't sign the papers, but I'm more or less doing the job," he said this week.

He's also traveled across the country to handle speaking engagements, including three within 24 hours in the middle of the week. He has spent considerable time learning the workings of the 38,000-employee Commerce Department, which promotes the nation's economic development and technological advancement.

That is why Hodges reacted with such concern upon learning the federal judge ruled the president can't enforce part of his voluntary wage and price guidelines.

"Theoretically, that takes the stick away from the president," said Hodges. "It would be nice if the carrot was enough, but it isn't always. Now the stick has been taken away because it might hurt somebody."

Hodges knows first-hand that the country faces very serious economic problems, the type that might cause widespread social change in the next few years. He also knows it's going to be part of his job to help solve them.

"I want to help Mr. Carter and I want to help this country," Hodges said shortly before speaking to an international trade conference here. "He is addressing the economic problems of today, but it's going to take him $5\frac{1}{2}$ years of work. It would take anybody that long. The Lord Himself would take that long."

The immensity of the problems is one of the reasons Hodges agreed to take the commerce department post.

"It is truly something meaningful," he said, while sipping on a glass of ice water. "I'll be dealing with trade and inflation and trying to improve the business climate."

Close friends of Hodges think it is the type challenge that will use his many talents to great advantage. They also admit privately that they are glad to see Hodges get the opportunity they feel he deserves.

The 42-year-old Charlottean quit a $125,000-a-year job with NCNB to run for the United States Senate. Those plans came to an abrupt and totally unexpected halt one year and three days ago when he lost to Insurance Commissioner John Ingram in a runoff election for the Democratic nomination.

Although his name was mentioned in connection with several federal or state posts, Hodges eventually chose to teach at Duke University. Nobody expected him to remain as a teacher there forever; Hodges was simply waiting for the right opportunity.

"A lot of people are saying that I'll be with the Commerce Department only a short time. That's not what I'm planning. I think I'm there as a manager to help administer the department," said Hodges, son of a former governor of North Carolina who also served as Commerce Secretary under President John Kennedy.

"I want to be considered a businessman still, but one who made a contribution in the public sector. I don't know how long that will last, but I view myself as a businessman involved in the public policy process.

Hodges has long said that businessmen must become involved in government.

"Business can't stay aloof from the public system," Hodges said this week. "Business has got to do things to better understand the public. Similarly, government has got to understand business."

The only way that will happen, he said, is to get businessmen and women involved in politics and the government. Hodges realizes, however, that will be a difficult task. There simply aren't that many executives willing to sacrifice $100,000-plus a year salaries for the $57,500 a U.S. senator makes each year or the $52,000 that the Commerce Department undersecretary makes.

That gamble is especially risky for somebody running for an elected office since there is no guarantee of winning. Hodges was forced to cash in investments and use personal savings to pay off a personal loan of more than $300,000 incurred during his Senate campaign.

"There's no doubt the financial aspect is the biggest burden," he said. "It is a dramatic sacrifice."

Hodges expects to spend a good bit of his time in the Commerce Department speaking to businessmen, trade groups and the like.

He said he has a "great" personal relationship with Commerce Secretary Juanita Kreps, whom he has known for many years. He was, in fact, the Kreps' banker in Chapel Hill at one time. In addition, Secretary Kreps was on the NCNB Corp. board of directors with Hodges before taking the Commerce position.

Secretary Kreps was a teacher and administrator at Duke University before taking the cabinet post.

"I think our relationship is a great asset for the Department of Commerce," Hodges said.

The pair will need any advantage they can get because there are monumental problems that must be addressed, including the imbalance between exports and imports, other trade problems, inflation and the dollar's slide in relation to foreign currencies.

And, there is always the energy situation, which will undoubtedly affect the Commerce Department because much of the country's trade imbalance is tied to petroleum imports.

"We've flat got a damn crisis," Hodges said. "It's no longer a technological problem. The technology is there, but the price has to be such (to make new methods attractive to oil and energy-related companies). Nationalizing the oil companies doesn't change that. It's now a political problem."

Hodges said people will simply have to learn to be satisfied with less energy than they've had in the past.

But there is still a question of whether people willingingly will accept less in a democracy, Hodges said.

"People may not vote for less today, but as the world grows around them, they will have to adapt to different standards."

Hodges does not think the U.S. can continue to "satisfy the economic machine we're used to."

"The American people want instant solutions," Hodges said. "When they don't get them, Carter becomes an S.O.B. Well, there are no instant solutions. I think the president is on the right track.

"The real problem with the dollar is that people don't have the guts to address the problem in the first place. I think some of the shocks we're getting are really very good. The trade and energy shocks are forcing this country to look again. Business has been so good recently that we didn't have to work as hard to get new markets, to understand other cultures. Once people start needing business, they'll start looking overseas."

One certainty is that Hodges will be facing problems considerably more complex and severe than the ones his father had to tackle when he led the department almost 20 years ago.

"I certainly never thought about succeeding him, but he certainly charted that path for me," Hodges said. "Mrs. Kreps had my father's portrait in the office when I came in. I didn't know whether to take it down or leave it up.

"I finally moved it to another wall. At least I'll have somebody to tell my Hodges jokes to who will enjoy them."

THE WASHINGTON POST TUESDAY, MARCH 5, 1985

RUDOLPH A. PYATT JR.

D.C. Banking's Voice

Senior management at Washington Bancorp and The United Mine Workers of America appear to be the obvious winners in the sale of the company and its principal subsidiary, The National Bank of Washington.

By selling the company, the UMW exchanges an admittedly unsatisfactory investment for greater financial security. For its part, Washington Bancorp's management guarantees itself a measure of security by becoming partners—if only minor ones—in the investor group that has agreed to buy the holding company and its subsidiary.

Considered in a different context, however, the transaction, which assures the retention of Washington Bancorp's senior management, also assures the banking community of retaining one of its most effective voices in the development of the industry and the region. Some might argue that, as a result, banking and local government are also winners in the NBW sale.

A D.C. government official indirectly raised the issue in a conversation last week by suggesting that Luther H. Hodges Jr., Washington Bancorp's chairman and chief executive officer, has emerged as the unofficial spokesman for the local banking community.

Some may disagree with the premise, but, the truth is, Hodges, in only four years as chairman and chief executive officer of NBW, has become the most visible and, arguably, the most effective articulator of banking's positions on regional business and economic issues.

To say that Hodges is the D.C. banking industry's leading spokesman may be an exaggeration, but there can be no question that he has firmly established himself as one of the District's most influential bankers. Not only is his input sought regularly by government and business leaders, but Hodges has positioned himself to affect decisions that have an impact on commerce in the region.

Once-familiar names from the banking community have given way to Hodges', for example, as vice president of the Greater Washington Board of Trade, immediate past chairman of the BOT's international business development committee, co-chairman of the Washington-Baltimore Regional Association and trustee of the Greater Washington Research Center. Hodges chaired Mayor Marion Barry's Downtown Committee and accompanied the mayor, as a representative of the private sector, on a trade mission to China last year.

Hodges defines the difference between a visionary and a banker oriented to the bottom line.

A member of Hodges' banking fraternity agrees with the premise posed by the District official last week. "They're right. It's not that [Hodges] is the spokesman for the bankers but, first of all, Luther is a politician and he understands the value of good public relations. He doesn't do it under the auspices of the [D.C.] bankers association but he sees a void and he has moved to fill it."

That is precisely what Hodges did recently in the matter of the simmering controversy surrounding a report which examined the relative competitive positions of banks in the region.

Privately, local bankers—indeed, the leadership of the D.C. Bankers Association—have taken exception to most of the findings in the report, which was done for the Greater Washington Research Center. But the DCBA has yet to challenge or endorse the report in a way that might be helpful to public understanding of the issue.

Hodges, on the other hand, saw a void and accepted the challenge presented by the report. In a rebuttal that was published in The Post last Sunday, he acknowledged that outside competition poses a "problem" for local banks. At the same time, however, Hodges offered readers a different perspective of the problem, while suggesting a possible scenario in which banking and economic development strategies might strengthen the industry here.

To be sure, some solutions that Hodges proposes are open to question. His well-known advocacy of a strategy that would make Washington an international financial center, for example, may be wishful thinking, given the realities of the makeup of the local private sector.

On the other hand, by taking a broader view of the region's economy in his overall approach to addressing the local banking industry's problems, Hodges defines the difference between a visionary and the bottom-line-oriented banker.

That much is clear in the continuing debate over the pros and cons of a financing package for a proposed commercial project in the Shaw community. Above all else, NBW's commitment stands up to scrutiny.

While larger D.C. banks were reluctant to finance the start of the project—notwithstanding a guarantee of repayment by the D.C. government—NBW agreed to be the lead bank in putting together the loan package. Under new management and new owners, NBW's commitment might have been different.

It's not difficult to understand why so many business and government leaders were interested in the sale of NBW.

83

WASHBIZ

RUDOLPH A. PYATT JR.

The Strife at Washington Bancorp

Last week's attempted coup at Washington Bancorp may have established new marks for hypocrisy and sheer *chutzpah*.

Power struggles have shaken the boardrooms of Washington banks before, but it's doubtful that any compare with the surprise attack on Washington Bancorp Chairman Luther H. Hodges Jr. by Saudi Arabian investors, who own more than 27 percent of the company's stock, and Robert B. Washington, a director of the company and partner in a Washington law firm.

In recent years, chief executives and prominent directors have been forced out at Riggs National Bank, American Security Bank and National Savings & Trust Bank (since merged into Crestar Financial Corporation). The campaign against Hodges, however, may be the unkindest cut of all. It was Hodges, ironically, who invited Washington and his allies in the campaign against him to join the company as director and investors. *Et tu Brute!*

Hodges apparently assumed that no one, certainly not Washington, would challenge him for control of the company and its principal subsidiary, National Bank of Washington. Hodges must have expected, nevertheless, that the Saudis would present some sort of challenge eventually. Insiders say Arab investors had expressed dissatisfaction over the direction in which Hodges was taking the company. It's no secret that Hodges hoped to make NBW attractive enough to become a potential merger partner.

Washington's campaign to oust Hodges is another matter. Hodges, after all, was Washington's chief sponsor, having invited him to serve first on NBW's board in 1981 and later as a director of the holding company. Indeed, Hodges supported Washington's nomination this year for another two-year term on the holding company's board, even though the two

This 1988 article summarizes the challenges facing the National Bank of Washington.

men had differed sharply over the propriety of retaining Washington as a director. Washington remained on the board even though the bankrupt law firm in which he was a comanaging partner—Finley, Kumble, Wagner, Heine, Underberg, Manley, Myerson & Casey—failed to repay NBW a $10 million loan.

In seven years as a director, Washington never publicly questioned Hodges' management of NBW. Now that the Finley, Kumble loan has become an issue, Washington refuses to accept responsibility for the loan either as a former member of the law firm or as a director who maintained less than arm's-length distance in his knowledge of the transaction. He blames Hodges, instead, for incompetence, among other things, not only for the bank's decision to underwrite the loan to Finley, Kumble, but also for NBW's overall performance.

Unquestionably, NBW's performance has been mixed since Hodges was named chairman in 1980. Still, under Hodges, NBW has come back a long way from the troubled institution that it was eight years ago when nonperforming insider loans and lack of internal controls threatened its viability and led to intervention by federal regulators.

Washington must have known that problem loans were a major reason for the bank's uneven earnings during his tenure as a director. Wafic Said, the principal stockholder, had to have been aware of them as well. In fact, the bank had $172 million in foreign loans at the end of 1983 and $117 million in 1985.

The bulk of those loans were made to Latin American countries whose liquidity problems have created a drag on earnings at banks all across the country. Washington Bancorp, like other bank holding companies in the region, was forced to boost loan loss reserves for Third World debt in the past couple of years.

Still, Washington Bancorp's assets have doubled in the past five years to more than $2 billion, with an annual growth rate of nearly 15 percent. That compares favorably with annual growth rates over the same span for several mid-size regional banks. Return on assets and return on equity, key measurements of bank performance, have not kept pace with those of more profitable banks, however.

In any event, Washington apparently had sufficient confidence in NBW to invest substantially more in the company's stock than he had during most of his tenure as a director. In the first five years as a director, he owned only 100 shares of NBW stock. Now he owns or controls about 5 percent, most of it purchased after 1985 during the peak of spirited interstate merger activity in the District.

Said and his associates also apparently had few misgivings about NBW and Hodges when they became the principal

continues

shareholders in 1985. Indeed, they approached Hodges through an intermediary to express their interest in becoming major shareholders.

The United Mineworkers of America, which had owned NBW since the 1940s, agreed to sell its controlling interest (76 percent) in 1985 to an outfit called Colson Inc. which was described then as a New York investment firm. Neither of the two investors who were identified then as principal owners of Colson ever owned much of NBW's stock, however. Colson was merely a vehicle for Said and his group.

Colson subsequently merged with Washington Bancorp, exchanging shares in a subsequent reorganization that reduced Said's stake in the company.

Washington and his allies, who were defeated by a majority of the bank company's board in their initial bid last week to topple Hodges, may differ with Hodges on a plan to make NBW more competitive, but they all know what the obstacles are. Not only was NBW experiencing difficulty with bad loans, including the one to Finley, Kumble, but it lacked the size to go out and buy a large franchise. Instead, it bought a small bank in Northern Virginia and is awaiting approval to buy a Maryland savings and loan and convert it to a commercial bank.

An expanded market, with access to deposits in both Virginia and Maryland, would ostensibly make NBW more attractive as a takeover target, but the reality is that NBW is in banking limbo. Interstate banking fever has subsided in the region. Foreign loans continue to be a problem and NBW continues to have a unionized work force. It's the only bank in the region whose employees are represented by organized labor, a carryover from the old days of UMWA ownership.

That, however, may not be as big an obstacle as some believe. In fact, recent improvement in earnings may have prompted an offer for the bank. Indeed, that may be one reason why the board has retained an adviser to study strategic alternatives.

No one will talk about a possible offer on the table, but selling the bank may be an acceptable alternative to further strife fueled by dissident stockholders. ∎

619 14TH STREET, N.W., WASHINGTON, D.C. 20005

NEWS RELEASE

FOR IMMEDIATE RELEASE:
APRIL 13, 1989

Washington D.C., April 13, 1989. Washington Bancorporation (WBC-D.C.; NASDAQ), parent company of The National Bank of Washington (NBW) and The Washington Banks in Virginia and Maryland, today announced that it had settled its outstanding litigation with its largest stockholder, Washington National Holdings, N.V. (WNH), and related persons and entities. All claims made by WBC and NBW against WNH, Wafic Said, Ziad Idilby, and Richard Bodman and related entities, and all counter-claims and cross-complaints made by the WNH defendants against WBC, NBW and officers and directors of WBC by WNH and related defendants, will be dismissed. No payment of damages or expenses by either side was involved in the settlement.

The WNH entities and WBC's board have agreed to work together, in full cooperation, to pursue the strategic alternatives being considered by a special board committee, which may include the sale of WBC. The parties have agreed that a definitive decision on a transaction should be made by year-end. The WNH entities have committed to support and participate in a transaction which meets certain parameters, including a separate sale of their interest in WBC at a price above the current market price.

The WNH entities have pledged their full support and cooperation to Luther H. Hodges, Jr., as Chairman and Chief Executive Officer of WBC and NBW. Mr. Hodges said, "I am delighted to announce this settlement, which I believe is in the interest of all of our shareholders. I want to especially acknowledge the personal commitment of Mr. Wafic Said who played an important role in making a favorable resolution possible."

continues

87

Hodges continued, "This is a 'win' for everybody. I am confident that, with the time to act prudently, the support of our largest shareholder, and our strong financial performance of last year and the first quarter of 1989, we will be able to present a transaction by year-end that will satisfy the stated objectives of both Mr. Said and the majority of our board. Mr. Said and his representatives have committed to cooperate in such a transaction. I am so confident of our ability to accomplish this that I have offered to step down as Chief Executive Officer as of January 1, 1990, unless asked to continue by our board, including the WNH representatives."

Ziad Idilby, one of the representatives of WNH on the boards of WBC and NBW, said, "We welcome this constructive resolution of all disputes between us and Mr. Hodges and the other directors. We are delighted to be able to announce our full support of Mr. Hodges and his management team as they complete the strategic assessment process which we agree should continue."

In connection with the settlement agreement, the Board of Directors of WBC has authorized an amendment to the shareholder rights plan adopted in October to satisfy WNH's concern that the plan might be interpreted to affect it adversely. Information as to this change will be mailed to shareholders shortly.

The annual meeting of WBC slated for April 28, 1989, will be held as scheduled and the Said interests have indicated that they will support the four nominees of the Board of Directors at that meeting.

NBW: Let's Get All the Facts
By Luther H. Hodges, Jr.

The Washington Post's editorial of August 4, 1990 attributed the fall of The National Bank of Washington to "years of misman-agement and internal quarrelling" and to "too many banks in this country to survive efficiently and profitably." To be sure, bank failures have increased greatly. As for the other matters, a fair account of NBW's own complex struggle would have been welcome. A proud community institution and its former employ-ees and shareholders deserve it.

The seeds of NBW's problems were planted twenty years ago, after the death of the legendary John L. Lewis and the retire-ment of his personal banker, Barney Colton, NBW's longtime Chairman. The Bank, owned by the United Mine Workers of America, changed management frequently throughout the 1970's. It engaged in heavy international lending that created problems later. It made no serious effort to adapt to new compe-tition in the era of deregulation. Its profitability then was largely maintained by the sale of bank-owned premises. Operating per-formance steadily declined, culminating in 1980 with charges of insider abuse. By today's standards, the Bank had failed and was ripe to be taken over by regulators.

When I assumed management in November 1980, the gov-ernment was sensitive to the fact of union ownership and was not inundated by other banking problems. Thus, the Comptroller of the Currency worked closely with the new management which, in turn, worked to rehabilitate the Bank. By 1985, the union was able to sell its interest to new investors for $70 million.

continues

[Op Ed submitted to *The Washington Post*, August 1990]

The Bank's recovery, never completed, was acknowledged in 1985 when the Comptroller of Currency removed the Bank from its "problem list," and it peaked with record earnings in 1988. The holding company's stock, worth $5 ½ in 1980, recorded a high of $25 ½ in 1986 and traded at $17 as late as March 1990. Bank employees toiled diligently to effect this turnaround and should rightfully be proud of their effort.

A number of underlying circumstances present in 1980 later matured into problems. The Bank had attempted to compete as a wholesale, not a consumer, institution. Its loan portfolio consisted of international loans, construction and interim real estate lending, and permanent mortgages at low, fixed rates. It was a District of Columbia bank unable, under then existing bank laws, to enjoy suburban opportunities which supported other banks. These circumstances and the evolution of U.S. banking rendered inevitable the Bank's sale to a larger institution.

The problems in NBW's international loans began to emerge. Government regulators decided in 1987 that the problems had crystallized sufficiently to require write-offs. Profitability was seriously affected. We tried to offset the international concentration by developing domestic corporate loans, but we were unsuccessful, and thus we expanded our real estate lending.

The Bank's real estate portfolio had traditionally been a strength, and in September 1989, bank regulators reviewed it without major criticism. Bank capital ratios, loss reserves, and lending policies had consistently been deemed by regulators to be at least adequate. However, the real estate market and related regulatory policy changed dramatically. In spring 1990, regulators discounted the prospect of real estate recovery and required reclassification of these loans. Precious capital was diverted to reserves for losses. This led to the holding company's posting a major loss.

I agree with the *Post* that the Bank's failure was not solely the result of decline in the economy or real estate. It reflected a combination of factors. In February 1988, the bankruptcy of a major law firm borrower triggered the largest loan default in the Bank's history. Further, the bitter fight for corporate control which erupted in October 1988 and was carried forth in the press, costly litigation, and the political process, undoubtedly took its toll in customer perceptions and our energies. No responsible corporate director should take grievances to the public without first bringing them to the Board of Directors. Moreover, after I resigned in January 1990, some questionable actions are alleged to have occurred regarding the holding company's commercial paper; these will be explored in the courts and elsewhere.

Banks fail because of some combination of inadequate government policy or regulation, fraud, changes in the business cycle, or mismanagement. NBW travelled its own particular path. Never in the last three decades has NBW been considered a particularly strong, profitable institution, but it was on the mend, and it boasted many loyal customers and employees—and a laudable record of community involvement and service of community banking needs. This all has been an expensive lesson, too important to be debated without a full understanding of all the facts.

****

[Luther H. Hodges, Jr. was Chairman of the Board of The National Bank of Washington from 1980 to January 1990, and of Washington Bancorporation from 1983 to January 1990.]

Send in the Clowns
by Luther H. Hodges, Jr.

There is—or was—a difference between commercial banks and savings and loan associations. Did Congress ever realize this difference? There is a conflict between strong financial institutions quite necessary in a growing economy in a globally competitive environment and a populistic distrust of moneyed interests. Does Congress appreciate this distinction? There is a difference between courageous political leadership and simply identifying bureaucratic scapegoats within the regulatory system. Does Congress understand? There is a difference between misfortune and fraud. Does our government know the difference?

Amidst all the talk about the failures of the banking system and the excesses of the 1980's, the debate has been strangely silent about the role of the U.S. Government—Congress, the GAO, and the regulatory agencies, but particularly, the Congress and its banking committees which have been singularly noted for a lack of financial leadership since the early decades of the 20th century. How did the Banking Insurance Fund improve from a negative position of $7.03 billion at year-end 1991 to an estimated surplus of $1.2 billion at the end of March 1993? Did bankers suddenly get smarter, or did the government suddenly realize that perhaps something had gone awry with banking legislation and regulation in the 1980's?

Take The National Bank of Washington (NBW) as one example of regulatory mismanagement—an institution founded in 1807, involved in the financing of the War of 1812 and a survivor

[Written in 1992 just prior to Federal Judge Royce Lamberth's decision in favor of the defendants with "criticism to the U.S. Government" for bringing the lawsuit.]

of other local and global conflicts plus the Great Depression, only to fail in the late summer of 1990 during the reconfirmation hearings of the then Comptroller of the Currency. NBW, the oldest bank in the nation's capitol and one with a fine record of community reinvestment, was confined to the boundaries of the District of Columbia and became largely dependent on real estate lending—not in the 1980's but throughout its modern history—because the driving, if not the sole, private sector force in the local economy was real estate. These facts were well known and well documented in countless regulatory examinations. What changed in the late 1980's was a regulatory attitude that suddenly demanded that problem loans be dumped and not rescheduled over a logical business cycle, as is presently being pursued in Japan.

Problem real estate assets brought down many banks and seriously exacerbated the recession of 1990–91. Similarly, earlier in the 1980's, banks in the farm belt failed during a serious agricultural recession, and Texas and Oklahoma banks failed during the domestic energy crisis. The traditional view that hometown banks know best their borrowers and the local economy does not really help when that local economy goes sour, and our government should, as every other government seems to do, encourage bank expansion and geographic diversification. Populism in banking was a 19th century phenomenon and 15,000 banks and 3,500 savings and loan associations simply did not make sense as the U.S. economy limped into the 1980's.

The problem originates with the Congress which seems to have never understood that banking is a key factor in economic growth and is not a bastion of special interests. The emerging savings and loan problem was "solved" in 1981 with far-reaching legislation, encouraged by a politically powerful savings and loan lobby, that permitted a dramatic expansion of S&L assets in order to cope with a serious crisis on the liability side of those balance sheets. Moreover, Congress throughout the 1980's ignored the logic of an expansion of bank services plus interstate banking, as other financial services companies successfully fought to significantly reduce the market share of the commercial banking industry.

Certainly, fraud existed in the comparatively unregulated savings and loan industry, but Congress attributed the same ethical standard to all, and the Senate Banking Committee, ironically chaired by one of the "Keating Five," became "purer than Caesar's wife" in promoting legislation in 1989, 90, and 91, authorizing and encouraging the FDIC and the RTC to aggressively pursue any director of any failed financial institution. The National Bank of Washington became one of the first commercial banks to become a target of the regulators armed with these new powers, and millions of dollars were spent by the FDIC in developing a case of fraud on the part of NBW officers and directors. In essence, private sector law firms were given dramatic incentives to bring law suits on behalf of the regulators, whose sole concern seemed to be whether Congress or the GAO would second-guess them.

The NBW case, described by the local press as a "legal fiasco" in which a "jury of fools" could have pointed out the FDIC's errors and inconsistencies, has now been totally dismissed by U.S. District Judge Royce Lambreth. The sanctions awarded against the government in this landmark case were traded away in order to avoid further litigation from a government seeking to "blackmail" any director who had assets which the FDIC could attack. That those same regulators now ponder why banks are reluctant to make loans only adds to the farcical nature of the situation.

Conveniently lost in the settlement of the NBW case was

any acknowledgement that the Saudi Arabian interests, which owned the controlling shares in the bank and dominated the management of the institution in the months prior to its failure, were at all accountable. Inexplicably, these individuals were not sued! I personally did what one assumes that the U.S. Government now says that it wanted Clark Clifford and Robert Altman to do in the case of BCCI and the First American Banks of Washington. I reported in 1988 to a disinterested Federal Reserve Board that a foreign owned bank holding company had violated, in the opinion of bank management—officers and a solid majority of the board of directors—securities laws and bank holding company regulations. The government ignored the request for an investigation, leaving the matter to the courts in the case just now settled, but that litigation severely weakened the bank as it expended in excess of $6 million in legal fees in 1988–89. The FDIC's private sector law firm chose to ignore the Saudi role in the bank, and, I believe, Prince Bandar Bin Sultan, the powerful Saudi Ambassador to the United States, protected his friends with his unique influence within the Bush Administration.

What Congress and the regulators should consider is how their own actions aggravated the banking problem. On closing NBW, the FDIC announced that the Bank Insurance Fund would absorb at least a $500 million loss, perhaps as much as $800 million. The FDIC, as receiver of NBW's assets, proceeded to sell and auction real estate and real estate loans during the absolute low-point for real estate values in the Washington area. Even with these depressed values, and after wasting millions of dollars in legal fees pursuing innocent people, selling to a foreign investor for $3 million an historic landmark valued at $15 million, refusing to compromise early on commercial litigation and losing $24 million plus millions more in legal fees to private sector law firms, offering deep discounts on loans that could have ultimately paid in full, the FDIC announced earlier this year that a loss of $150 million was expected. This loss is approximately one half of that which former FDIC Chairman L. William Seidman would have predicted when he stated that the assets are discounted 20% as soon as the government steps in. Was the Bank Insurance Fund ever really broke? Or were regulators, dogged by Congress and the GAO, so afraid of underestimating losses that they simply "blew it" with NBW and many other financial institutions?

I believe the government owes an explanation to the countless officers and directors in banking throughout the country who have been harassed by federal regulators—not to mention the shareholders and employees of The National Bank of Washington and other institutions who would never have lost their investment or their jobs had their own government truly understood the business it was regulating.

Luther Hartwell Hodges, Jr. (born November 19, 1936) is a retired American businessman. He was the first United States Deputy Secretary of Commerce (1980–81), appointed under President Jimmy Carter. Hodges was the chairman of the North Carolina National Bank as a member of the "aggressive and youthful" management of the bank that led to it becoming the largest bank in the Southeast. He was the president of the Charlotte Chamber of Commerce in 1976 and later became the president-elect of the Greater Washington Board of Trade. He was chairman of Washington Bancorporation, the parent company of The National Bank of Washington, for ten years, until he resigned in January 1990. Hodges moved to Santa Fe, New Mexico, and became the owner/publisher of *The Santa Fean Magazine* and is currently an owner of the Hotel Santa Fe. He subsequently relocated to Chapel Hill, North Carolina, where he was an adjunct professor at the Kenan-Flagler Business School. He has been a member of the Board of Governors of the University of North Carolina, along with similar service to The College of Santa Fe, the American University, and Johnson C. Smith University. He is also the author/co-author of a number of books on business education. He has served on the board of directors of numerous corporations and civic organizations, and his personal investment company, Phoenix Associates, Inc. is also involved with many entrepreneurial businesses and venture capital opportunities. He was educated at the University of North Carolina (BA, 1957) and Harvard Business School (MBA, 1961). He served to the rank of Lieutenant, United States Naval Reserve (1957–65).

Made in the USA
San Bernardino, CA
20 September 2016